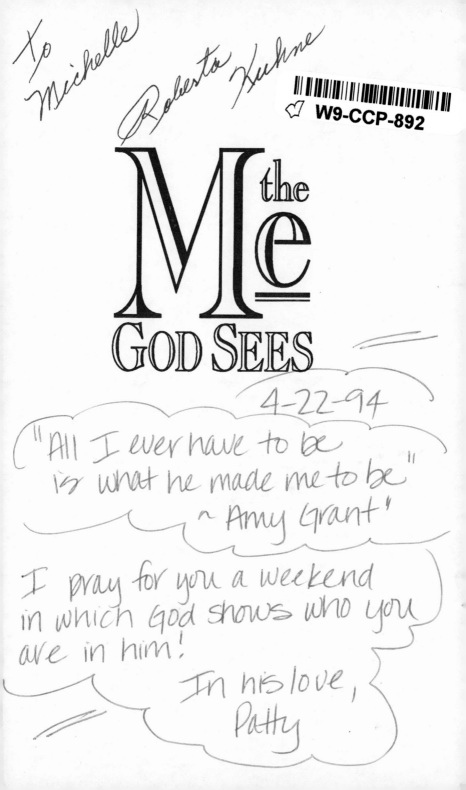

To
Michelle

Roberto Kuhne

W9-CCP-892

# M the e
# GOD SEES

4-22-94

"All I ever have to be
is what he made me to be"
~ Amy Grant"

I pray for you a weekend
in which God shows who you
are in him!

In his love,
Patty

# Me the

# GOD SEES

*Celebrating Your True Identity*

# Roberta Kuhne

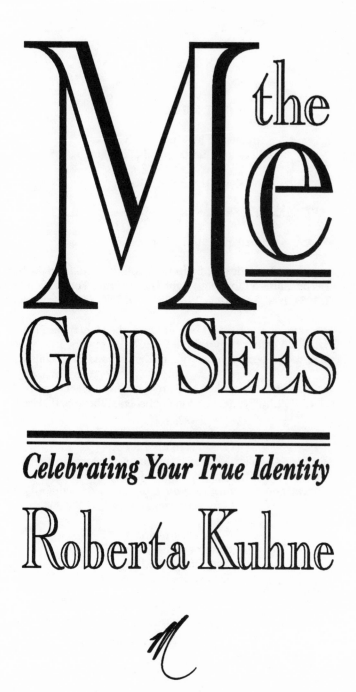

THE ME GOD SEES

published by Multnomah Books
part of the Questar publishing family

© 1993 by Roberta Kuhne

International Standard Book Number: 088070-573-6

Printed in the United States of America

For information:
Questar Publishers, Inc.
Post Office Box 1720
Sisters, Oregon 97759


93 94 95 96 97 98 99 00 01 — 10 9 8 7 6 5 4 3 2 1

# DEDICATION

To my Robert.
You are the wind beneath my wings.

To my Sequoia Sisters,
Linda, Kathleen, Cathy, and Sheryl,
whose roots grow deep into Living Waters.

# CONTENTS

# Before You Begin

Question: If you could be anyone in the world, who would you be?

Answer: The me God sees.

This has been my personal pursuit and purpose in writing this book—to learn about and see ourselves as God sees us. He holds a picture of us before Him that is the fulfillment of His plans, purposes, and potential for our lives. This is the me God sees.

Within the pages of this book, I have tried to encourage you to think why you may have feelings of worthlessness or inadequacy, where those feelings originated, and what to do about them. My aim is for you to discover your true identity and celebrate the unique way God made you.

I strongly recommend you answer the study questions at the end of each chapter. They will challenge you to think the truth about yourself, and then live it. Don't miss this important part of the book. Gather with your friends and do this study together. You'll laugh, weep, and grow together, but you will never be the same once you grasp a glimpse of the person God sees! Why? Because He sees a different me than I see, and it's a wonderful portrait!

I made a wonderful discovery in writing this book. Books don't just happen! There is sacrifice, solitude, scribbling, and sweat. In the midst of it all I had much help to complete this work. My sincere thanks to...

My editor Carol Bartley, who skillfully read my scribbling and sifted, shortened, shredded, suggested, and summarized. Sure enough she stuck it out with me! How grateful I am for having the privilege of working with this talented, discerning editor who made me rethink and rewrite! Carol, I proudly present to you the coveted Editorial Genius Award of 1993— the sequined baseball cap! I know you secretly want one.

Larry Libby who listened to me in the beginning with his heart. You understood the message I wanted to convey. You believed in me!

John Politan for his tireless efforts on behalf of this book. Within his incredibly busy schedule that includes his law practice, seminary, Sunday school teaching, and his wife Terri, John always found time to read, pray, and comment on the latest chapter I agonized over. Terri's faithful prayers and uplifting words of kindness brought me through many a day. Words alone cannot contain the measure of my appreciation to both of you.

All forty-seven of my prayer partners. I give you my heartfelt gratefulness.

My secret pal, whoever you may be. You cheered me with your notes, delighted me with your gifts, and comforted me with the knowledge of your persevering prayers. Your kindnesses always seemed to arrive at just the right moment.

Tim Kimmel, who gets the world class award for encouragement! "Roberta, you've got a book here. This time next year, you'll be an author! God placed a book in your heart, and you must write it." You helped me see greater potential in myself than I saw. Tim, you were the impetus that got me into this. You said, "Writing a book is like giving birth to barbed wire!" You were right!

My Sequoia Sisters—Linda Bender, Kathleen Hall, Cathy Schadt, and Sheryl Wueste—who listened to me, prayed for me, lifted my burdens, carried my concerns, and loved me through it. You are treasured!

Shannon, our daughter who lived with us during this writing project. You disagreed with me frequently, wept with me often, laughed with me more, talked with me endlessly, lunched with me tirelessly, and loved me deeply. I am proud to have you as my daughter. I'll always hold your words deep in my heart, "Mom, no matter how many birthdays I have, you'll always be older!"

Robert, my extraordinary husband, lovingly called "Adorable" by me, laughingly called "Adorable" by our friends! Thank you for your endless patience, for all the interruptions with my latest ideas, for all the night trips to "get away" for a yogurt, for rides into the desert, for carefully listening to my thoughts at two in the morning, for long writing days and longer nights, for loving me so unconditionally. You are the best of the best. I could want for no more than you.

# 1

## The Master Designer Captures My Heart

The day of my birth was a truly grand event. I emerged from my dark, cozy place, where I didn't always get to choose the menu, to be greeted by bright lights, cameras, and many "oohs" and "ahs." I'm quite sure I heard someone say, "Isn't she wonderful?" At least that's what registered in my baby brain. It was probably my mother. Mothers say those things, you know. It doesn't make them any less true! And of course I believed whatever my mother said, until age thirteen.

When I arrived home, I was greeted by twin sisters who were considerably older than I. Fifteen months older to be exact. They would show me the ropes. Oh yes, Mother said they were wonderful, too.

Mother often dressed Joan and Joyce, the twins, alike. And, let's face it, they were cute. They didn't have to do anything but just sit there in the buggy and look adorable. It presented a problem when I tightened the turning room in the buggy by joining them with my frilly dresses and my beloved bonnets.

Passersby would gush, "Oh look, twins." Then the usual accolades would follow. My baby brain would be reeling. What about this curly-headed blonde in the rear of the buggy? I wondered and pushed myself forward.

In my preschool years I became wise to the ways of the world. Like most children, I enjoyed attention, and I noticed the twins were receiving a great deal of that precious commodity. I decided that there were different ways to get it. I just needed to learn the system.

That's when I decided to talk early and talk a lot. People can't ignore you when you're continually asking them questions. And talk I did. An incessant waterfall of words spilled over my lips from the rising of the sun to the setting of the same. I made my family crazy.

An important lesson was being learned: I had to earn attention and my sisters didn't. Honestly, I don't ever remember being insanely jealous of them. My mother's words, "Isn't she wonderful?" rang in my ears and became a song in my heart. She believed in me and so did my father.

For some strange reason that same expression was lavished on my sisters, but the song had a different melody from mine. Joan and Joyce were jocks. (We called them "tomboys" in those days.) They loved rough and tumble games, and I was a prissy little thing. I considered playing dolls, dress-up, and tea parties as my life's work. As the years unfolded, so did our unique personalities. Joyce and Joan entered their teen years as quiet and shy, except when playing sports. I was the exact opposite. I was all bubble, bluster, and babble.

## LOOKING FOR "IT"

To some, I may have appeared to have it all together, but God had some serious work to do in my life. As a young girl about to enter college, I was very insecure and had a burning desire to feel worthwhile. So, the age-old questions surfaced in my life, "Who am I really?" "Do I really matter?" "What is my purpose in life?" "Where did I come from?" "Where am I going?"

What is it that will answer these questions? What is "It"? All my life I had been looking for "It." You know what "It" is. "It" is the answer to these questions. You've been looking for "It" too. Some of us search all of our lives and never look in the right places. Let me share with you how I found "It."

In high school I knew that if I could just make the pompom team that would be "It." After weeks of aerobic activity, bouncing, jumping, and leaping in my second floor bedroom (above the dining room), I made the pompom team. My mother probably thought, "Oh terrific, now she'll be practicing till she's on Medicare." (My parents noted that perhaps I was a bit obsessive.) What fun we all had, swinging five pounds of crepe paper in each hand. Then there was the night of the "big crash."

At half-time we were running onto the basketball court from the four corners. Trust me, it was a major production. We were to alternate and pass each other in the middle of the court. But one of the girls was practicing for *Chariots of Fire* (twenty years before they made it a movie) and running like the Olympian Eric Liddell—with her eyes closed and her head thrown back. Guess whom she crashed into and left sprawling on the floor?

You know what? Making the pompom team wasn't "It."

If only I could be Homecoming Queen my senior year. Not an uncommon wish for a young woman.

Wouldn't that be "It!" When the votes were counted and I won, I was elated. Homecoming weekend was a wonderful memory—the parade, the game, the dance. It all came and went so fast. But on Monday morning I realized I was just the former Homecoming Queen. That's all. I went around singing Peggy Lee's favorite oldie, "Is That All There Is?" My high school wish just wasn't quite "It."

My search continued into college, career, and beyond, always a quest for that elusive "It." Finally, I was sure my search for fulfillment and self-worth had ended. Why hadn't someone told me about this before? I knew what "It" was—"marriage." That was it!

Oh to have all my dreams completed in one man. He would fulfill my every need, longing, and deep yearning of my heart. We would be together all the time. I'd never have another lonely moment. Of course he'd always be there to encourage, comfort, and cheer. He'd be my biggest fan and take full responsibility for building up my self-esteem.

When children came along, naturally he'd be "Father of the Year." He'd come home from work and see that I'd had a tough day with the kids. "Honey, you just go lie down for a while. I'll fix dinner, change the baby, walk the dog, clean out the gerbil cage, and put the kids to bed." I have very vivid dreams.

Marriage for me was going to be for keeps, for real, for good, and forever. Period. Well, I met the man of my dreams, we were married in a fairy tale wedding with a honeymoon in Paris (airline employees), and he gave me two beautiful, wonderful children.

## MARRIAGE ISN'T "IT"

But my expectations came crashing down to earth with the power of a meteorite, smashing all my hopes and aspirations. One day my husband came to me and said, "Roberta, I don't love you anymore and I want a divorce." (That's when you leap off the rug, because it's being pulled from underneath you.) There was someone else in his life, and he wanted to marry her.

This couldn't be happening to me! I'd always been cherished by my parents. I was one of my father's favorite five children. The only man I'd ever been intimate with was rejecting me. Didn't want me, didn't need me, and didn't think I was "wonderful" at all.

Have you ever been so deeply hurt that it's all you think about? You climb into bed at night and slip under the covers with a fifty-pound weight on your chest. You can't believe they make such heavy blankets, but then you're aware, very aware, that it's the burden on your mind and the pain in your heart that's weighing you down. Sleep won't come. Thoughts of failure, rejection, inadequacy, and inferiority play reruns in your head all night. I hate those movies. Tears? Oh yes, plenty of them. I didn't know a woman my size could hold so much water. You can't eat, sleep, work, or believe that this pain will ever end. Some of you know exactly the kind of anguish I am talking about.

I had absolutely no sense of self-worth. After all, my former husband didn't want me, and I was convinced no one else did either. I began looking for "It" again—in all the wrong places, all the wrong faces, and all the wrong arms. That kind of life never builds up one's sense of self-esteem; it only destroys it. I wasn't the mother I wanted to be; I wasn't the person I had hoped to become. Here was a woman desperately wanting to be valued and cherished but digging her own pit, only to make a swan dive into the cesspool of despair.

## MY BEST FRIEND ROBERT

The airline I worked for promoted me to a public relations position in Chicago where my family lived. In my position I dealt with business people, celebrities, actors, actresses, politicians, and other VIPs. I met interesting people, traveled to exotic destinations, and learned a lot about famous "empty" lives.

It was here I met the man who was to become my husband. Now, Robert wasn't exactly what I was looking for. You see, I thought that a tall Tom Cruise would make an excellent husband. What wisdom I had. But Robert was different. If we were to conduct a General Norman Schwarzkopf look-alike contest, my Robert would win hands down.

Well, this Robert would not leave me alone. He was ubiquitous; he was absolutely everywhere! I really wasn't that interested; I wanted to pursue other things, but he sought after me and never seemed to tire.

Robert and I became good friends, the best of friends. It's been a lot of years now, but Robert is still my very best friend. I'm crazy about that man! Robert was strong where I was weak. He was wise where I was foolish. He was indeed the "wind beneath my wings." Also, he was financially sound and I was flat broke! He was always bailing me out of my troubles. As Robert once said, "Roberta, I had to marry you. I had such a financial investment in you, I couldn't afford to let you go." Now mind you, Robert did not come without some encumbrances and problems of his own, but he is perfect for me. Not perfect, but perfect for me.

We moved to Sacramento, California, where I went back to school to study art and interior design. I was sure this was "It." I had the love of a wonderful man, my children had a home, and I was back in college. I was knee-deep in pottery clay, oil paints, textiles, and art history and loving it. I thought I finally knew who I was and that I mattered, but something was still missing.

## HOW MY WORLD VIEWED CHRISTIANS

A woman named Marty threw pots with me in pottery class. (We didn't actually throw them at anyone; that's just a term for forming a pot on a potter's wheel.) A sign-up sheet was going around the classroom for a glassblowing class, and I asked Marty to go with me. Marty said, "I'm very sorry, but I'm busy that day." "Busy?" I said. "What could you possibly be doing that is more important than glassblowing?"

Marty at first didn't want to tell me; perhaps she thought I would ridicule her. Finally she said, "I attend a Bible study on that day." "A Bible study!" I exclaimed. "Can't you read it just once? Why would you want to study it over and over?" Then she said a very interesting thing: "I'm going to study the Bible until I meet its Author." I must tell you that intrigued me. She actually believed that the Bible was the Word of God.

For several weeks I pursued the subject, but Marty didn't invite me to her Bible study. She was a wonderful woman and didn't want to push me. But my desire to find out what went on at one of those

19

Friendship Bible Coffees got the best of me. I announced one day that I was going to invite myself.

Now, I knew I couldn't be a "real Christian" like those ladies. You see, I wore makeup and jewelry, and bleached my hair. Not only that, but I loved to laugh. You know how somber those Christians are. I couldn't become one of them, sitting around straightfaced and straightlaced, reading the Bible for hours on end while adjusting their aprons and smoothing their hair nets and buns! Why then, I wondered, did I feel compelled to attend this Bible study? Here were all these "holy women," no doubt poverty-stricken because their churches were always passing the collection plate. We'd all probably sit on the floor, since I had heard they lived simply.

But God has a way of meeting us where we are. He knew me better and more intimately than I knew myself. He knew how to get my attention, not just outwardly, but in the deepest recesses of my soul. He was lovingly drawing me to Himself. Despite all that was going well in my life, there was still a hunger in my heart and a restlessness in my inner being. I just didn't know that it was for God.

When Wednesday morning came, I decided to skip glassblowing and found myself driving up to one of the most beautiful homes in Hidden Valley to attend my first Bible study. I was getting dangerously close to "It."

You wouldn't believe the reception I was given as I entered that home. What beautiful women. How warm, how welcoming, how joyful. I felt a presence and peace there I had never experienced before. They loved me just because I was there and breathing. I listened as women shared their struggles, their pain, their joys, and their prayers. But best of all they read from the Book by that famous Author. And I became strangely warmed as I listened.

Priscilla, who was leading the study, left quite an impression on me. She talked about Jesus as if she knew Him. It was as though she had a personal relationship with God. I had never heard of such a thing, and I had sat in the pews at church all my life. Priscilla was enthusiastic, lighthearted, and full of life. My misconceptions were being washed away like dust in a sudden, summer cloudburst.

## I Did It "My Way"

It was here that I first began to grapple with the idea of sin. Of course I had heard that we were all sinners. But I didn't think I was expected to really believe it! I knew some real sinners, but I certainly wasn't one of them. After all, I was a good person; I didn't murder, steal, or hijack airplanes. Compared to all the lowdown characters in the world I looked pretty good. It was as if I thought God graded on a curve.

But I learned what sin really was—independence from God. With clenched fist I had been shaking my arm at God and saying, "God, I know your laws and your commandments, but I'm going to do it my way. "My Way." There isn't a person alive who hasn't done it "My Way." We want to be our own god; we don't want to acknowledge a supreme being. Good grief! We might have to answer to Him!

Sin, I learned, was self-centeredness, selfishness, hate, greed, envy, gossip, slander, jealousy, prideful arrogance, bitterness, drunkenness, gluttony, an unforgiving attitude, and more. Well, I was certainly guilty of a number of offenses on that list. And some of those sins were actually fun. Rats! Now think about it. If sin were hard work, would we bother? I think not. Sin is fun or we wouldn't pursue it with such fervor.

Ever notice how we don't want to call sin "sin"? We give it pretty, socially acceptable names. You're not drunk; you've just been "overserved." You're not selfish; you just have to "look out for number one." You're not committing adultery; you're having a beautiful, meaningful relationship. We need to call it what God calls it, and He calls it "sin." I had tried in the past to change my ways, but eventually I'd give in to temptation. What I needed was a power greater than myself. I needed to be forgiven. I needed a Savior.

I learned in that Bible study that only by faith in Him could I ever hope to gain heaven. Jesus Christ paid the debt for my sin and yours on the cross. Don't ask me how He took the sins of the world upon Himself that Good Friday. It's beyond my comprehension, but I believe it. If you and I were the only two people on earth, Jesus Christ would have come down to die just for us. And if you were the only one, He would have come for you. I was beginning to see that God puts a greater value on human life than we do. I began to view myself and others with new eyes.

## A CHOICE TO MAKE

These women took Jesus seriously. They weren't discussing religion; they were talking about a relationship with God. Then I read it; I saw it with my own eyes in the Gospel of John. Jesus claimed to be God! The Gospel of John is filled with the claims of Christ. If Jesus Christ claimed to be God, then He was not just a good man, not just a moral teacher, not just a prophet. I had a choice to make. I would either believe He was God or that He was a deceitful, despicable liar who also happened to be mad. Anyone who did and said what Jesus did was either the Son of God as He claimed or out of his mind. I wrestled with this choice. Couldn't I just settle for some "middle of the road" position? But Jesus didn't leave that option open to us. No other ways, no other choices. Just one way.

God created us with a vacuum inside, and we try all our lives to fill it. I was just wanting to find something, anything, that fit. It was like trying to fill the Grand Canyon with spoonfuls of earth, one at a time. The vacuum was too big, too grand, and my futile attempts, my answers to the dilemma, didn't fit. I was still searching for "It." Was it money, power, success, career, children, marriage, physical fitness, tennis, golf, or other pursuits? I'd push and shove to make these things fill that vacuum, but nothing did. You know why? It was God-shaped. Only God was meant to fill it. St. Augustine once said, "You (God) made us for Yourself and our hearts find no peace until they rest in You."[1]

That defined my feelings exactly—no peace. I thought I had all I needed to be happy and content in this life, but I didn't have what those women had. After I had been attending the Bible study for a couple of weeks, I began to hear these inner promptings. Not audible voices, but I was definitely hearing a message. Then one evening while I was studying for a French midterm, someone began speaking to me. The voice was one I could hear only with my heart, not my ears.

I didn't know it then, but it was the Holy Spirit speaking to my heart. "Roberta, it's time to commit your life to Jesus Christ." I listened and thought, Where did that come from? Besides, I don't want to do anything like "commit" (powerful word) my life to Jesus. Everybody knows what happens to people who do that. God sends them to Africa as missionaries! Nope, not me. I'll just attend that Bible study with those lovely women and read that great Book by that famous Author, and I'll be just fine.

God had other plans for me. He knew that on my own I wouldn't be just fine. That night I felt His presence in my room, in my heart, in my mind, and in my soul. There was no escaping Him. He was the perfect lover searching for His beloved, speaking words of promise, mercy, forgiveness, love, peace, and joy. He would not tire, nor give up, and He seemed to be everywhere I turned. He was ubiquitous, omnipresent. How could I turn my back on love like His? He shed His blood for love of me.

## I FOUND "IT"

I knew the historical Jesus; in fact, I even believed that He died on a cross and rose again on the third day. But I never believed He was who He said—God. I never called Him by His name—Jesus. Too personal, too intimate. I never trusted Him with my life, my heart, or my eternal destiny until that night. He was asking me to do that very thing—to surrender my will to Him. I never really "knew" Him until that night. Jesus has a way of making Himself irresistible to those who are searching for truth. I can best describe my encounter with God with these words, "Jesus captured my heart that night and has held it in His hand ever since."

I had found "It." I found that I mattered to God. I realized that my true value and worth was found in God's opinion of me. And to think that all these years I had been at the mercy of the world to give me an identity. I discovered that I could not truly know who I was apart from knowing Jesus Christ. No longer did I have to continually look to others for significance. I could look to God. And He thinks I'm a woman of worth. Have you found that you matter to God?

## LOVE NOTE TO GOD

Dear Lord, how I thank You for seeking after me. You have been faithful; I have been faithless. You have been forgiving; I have been unforgiving. You have given unconditional love; I have given conditional love. I desire to be like You. Teach me, dear Jesus, to walk in Your footsteps.

Love,
Me

## TELLING YOURSELF THE TRUTH

1. What circumstances, things, or people did you think would be "It" in your life? What happened?

2. What are you doing today to earn approval and acceptance? Are you receiving it? Is it worth it?

3. What is your first memory of your identity? Was it accurate? Who or what caused you to come to this conclusion?

4. Have you ever been lost in the wilderness, in a strange city, in a building, etc.? Did you know you were lost? Describe how you felt. How were you

found or how did you get out? Why do you think Jesus refers to nonbelievers as "lost"?

5. What would you say is man's greatest problem? What do you think God would say about man's greatest problem?

6. If you were God, how would you communicate to people? How does God communicate to people? Have you ever experienced communication with God?

7. What was the best decision you ever made in your life, apart from knowing God? Describe the circumstances. Did you seek the advice of others or did you act on your own? Do you think that God gives advice to His people? How?

8. What person in your life always seemed to know what was best for you? Do you honestly think God knows what is absolutely best for you? Why? Describe a time in your life when you did it "My Way," and it was definitely not "God's Way."

9. Describe a person in your life that you have deeply trusted. How did you come to trust him or her? Explain the difference between faith and trust. At what point does trust become faith? What is the difference between trusting Jesus Christ and placing one's faith in Him?

10. Have you ever had a major turning point in your life? Describe your experience. How has it changed your life?

# 2

## WINNING THE WORLD'S APPROVAL

W hat do you do, Roberta?" the aggressive, hard charging, tough-as-nails, professional woman asked me. Actually it was more like a challenge. The question wouldn't have been so threatening except that she was well aware I did not work outside the home. What did I do? I was a swimmer, a gardener, a speed walker, an artist of sorts, a dressmaker, and a Bible study teacher, but I wasn't sure she would believe any of those pursuits were worthy of discussion. Besides, that isn't who I am—my character, my heart, my soul. I decided to tell her I was writing a book. I had been thinking about it and collecting a few notes, quotes, and anecdotes, so it seemed like a good reply. She was satisfied. (How good that I was not wasting away at home doing the things I loved doing.) In her mind, only if I had accomplishments behind my name was I of worth.

"You don't use any night eye cream?" The cosmetic saleswoman was aghast as she moved in so close to me I could smell her mascara. "My, you look good for your age," she said—as if she were commenting on some interesting antique. (Translate that: "How wonderful. After all that wear and tear she can still manage to stand up.") "We'll have to soften those fine lines around your eyes and puff up those cells." She was out to intimidate me as she stared intently, looking for a weak link in my armor. "Aha! We have just the cream for that nasty scar on your neck." I'm thinking, What scar? I was beginning to lose all sense of security in who I was. Then I remembered the tiny scar. Her microscopic eyes magnified flaws that no ordinary mortal could detect. Good eyesight for a woman her age, I thought. She used words on me like "hygrascopic elements and natural ceramides," "tropocollagen and hyaluronic acid." I was impressed. She was gaining ground. How could I pass up all those secret ingredients I couldn't pronounce? In them surely lay the fountain of youth. Of course I would purchase these wonder creams. She approved, the skin care company approved, and the world approved. If MasterCard approved, we were in business! No doubt this would reverse the entire aging process twenty years!

But as I emerged and the light of day struck my "finely lined" eyes, I thought, Why did I believe her? How could I have bought into her balderdash? I know better than that. Why can't I accept the way God made me, with the character lines I've earned, and feel free to be me? The real me has an identity that has nothing to do with maturity, menopause, or midlife. It lies deep within my relationship with the Lord, not on the flawed surface.

What is the cry of your heart today? Perhaps, if only you knew that you were of great value, if only in the deepest reaches of your being you could feel good about how God made you, if only you had a healthy sense of self-worth, if only you felt treasured, if only someone esteemed you, if only you could be free to be all the person God planned for you to be! If only, if only! What if you could experience all of these things and the only requirement would be to tell yourself the truth? Tell myself the truth? Is that all? It sounds far too simple. Yet some of the greatest transformations and successes in life have been the result of one simple decision, one simple act, one simple commitment. When we take this message into our heart, not just our head, it profoundly changes our life. In fact, some of us will never be the same!

The words *self-esteem*, *self-worth*, *self-image*, and *self-concept* are somewhat similar, in that they describe how we feel and think about ourselves. For the most part, I will use them interchangeably. My purpose is not to exhaust the nuances of their definitions, but to target the root problems of these terms and to present a biblical view of you and me—the people that God sees. Let's examine the sources of self-esteem—the world's and perhaps yours.

## THE NEW RELIGION OF BEAUTY

Unfortunately, a woman's sense of self-esteem is frequently determined by her attractiveness. The slightest imperfection or physical flaw makes her feel inadequate.

Men, for the most part, are much different; they do not put such great emphasis on physical appearance. A woman can spend all day at the beauty salon having a manicure, coloring her hair, and receiving a pedicure, facial, and maybe even a massage. A man spending his day doing the same thing is under suspicion by other men. Oscar Wilde in his *Lecture on Art* states, "Of course, men don't age any better physically. They age better only in terms of social status. We misperceive in this way since our eyes are trained to see time as a flaw on women's faces where it is a mark of character on men's. If men's main function were decorative and male adolescence were seen as the peak of male value, a 'distinguished' middle-aged man would look shockingly flawed."

Today women are often thought of as "decorative." We are continually bombarded by unreasonable beauty standards, and we have participated in the problem by forming and embracing our own religion and belief system based on beauty. Naomi Wolf in her book *Beauty Myth* speaks of the Church of Beauty, which is a cultlike methodology to fill a spiritual void just as completely as traditional religion. It's much like the cult that sequesters and brainwashes its followers. She states, "The Rites of Beauty are able to isolate women so well because it is not yet publicly recognized that devotees are trapped in something more serious than a fashion and more socially pervasive than a private distortion of self-image."[1]

This new religion has spread rapidly as God has been replaced by the new altars of worship—the cosmetic counters. A "beauty god," who is tender, loving, and caring, offers "regeneration" to the aging woman. He is mindful of your needs and will offer a "balm" like Gilead's to soothe and comfort irritation. He gives "More Care," "Pure Care," "Natural Care," "Loving Care," and "Intensive Care." This god is long-suffering, providing Empathy shampoo, Kind cleanser, Caress soap, and Plenitude conditioner. He offers himself to you in a lipstick with which "you can have a lasting relationship."[2]

Of course this god will protect you from unseen dangers. You will be "shielded from...the elements" (Elizabeth Arden). "An invisible shield" will "alleviate years of negative influence" (Estée Lauder). You will be well supplied with "a protective barrier against external aggressors" (Charles of the Ritz).[3]

And what god does not call for sacrifice? The hundreds of dollars spent on miracle creams and holy oils is the sacrifice one willingly makes for her sins, for the wrinkles she fears will condemn her. If she fails to buy the creams and therefore ages, she obviously has not made the proper sacrifices.

What religion is complete without fasting? In the Church of Beauty women do not fast for spiritual reasons, but for thinness. Their god is an ultrathin idol who demands they starve themselves in order to be loved and accepted. Did you know that humans are the only creatures who refuse to eat when they are hungry and willingly starve themselves when surrounded by plenty? It is a self-denial ritual which includes fasting, starving, and sometimes even purging in search of a new self. The Church of Beauty is only interested in the continual pursuit of bodily perfection, and we have literally bought into its philosophy.

## "THIN AS A GLAMOUR MODEL"

Patti was nicknamed "fatty Patti" by her schoolmates. It was a familiar taunt during most of her adolescent years, and she grew to abhor it. She "would show them" one day! Patti was an easy mark for anorexia nervosa. She simply wanted to look "exactly like the models in *Glamour*." These women were given identities like "valued," "adored," "beautiful," and even "worshiped." Patti thought she knew just how to receive that same attention. She adopted a new identity for herself—"thin as a *Glamour* model."

When Patti was sixteen, it seemed reasonable to Patti's mother to encourage her daughter's self-imposed diet. After all, she was at least twenty pounds overweight. How good Patti would feel about her new image when she returned to high school next fall. The summer went smoothly with Patti taking on this new challenge with a vengeance. She started jogging and loved it, so that not a day would pass without her "little run." Taking the car into town was soon abandoned in favor of jogging the four miles each way, each day. And oh how she enjoyed tennis, especially singles. Where did she get all that energy, her mother wondered. Though her parents loved her and were devoted to her, it wasn't enough to contradict the message of the world. True acceptance for Patti was in pleasing the "noisier" world's message: "You can never be too thin." Thinness and exercise became obsessions for Patti. She lost forty pounds but still viewed herself as "fatty Patti."

I remember when I first saw her. I couldn't stop staring at her legs. Her thighs were as small as my upper arms! Her flesh was transparent and veined, her eyes shallow and sunken. Huge clumps of hair were missing from a once golden-haired woman.

Her senior year in college she was again admitted to the hospital. At five feet eight inches tall, ninety pounds and dropping, she was not going to live. A groundswell of concern and prayer went up for this young woman. "Thin as a *Glamour* model" became a death knell in her parents' ears. She would die if her body didn't respond soon. Fortunately, it did respond, and Patti lived to tell about the horrors of being at the mercy of the world's approval and the prison of her own unhealthy self-image. Today Patti is happily married and works as a counselor for eating disorders.

## WE'VE BOUGHT THE LIE

So many women have bought the lie that our value is based on our beauty or our thinness, the lie that our bodies define our beauty and our beauty defines our identity, our worth, and our self-esteem. We are quite familiar with the old adage regarding the sureness of death and taxes. But there is another nonnegotiable in life: We must live in our bodies for our entire time on earth. Yet our television sets, magazines, and advertisements continually remind us of the imperfections of this temple of ours.

Ever really listen to the TV commercials? What an absolute disgrace to have rough, red hands, dry, lifeless hair, or possibly none at all. How appalling to have those horrid age spots, zits, short nails, more than an inch to pinch around the middle, unsightly wrinkles, coffee-stained teeth, iron-starved blood, and not enough fiber in our diets.

Like the newlywed couple on their honeymoon. He took his bride by the hand and said, "Now that we're married, dear, I hope you won't mind if I mention a few little defects that I've noticed about you." "Oh, not at all," replied the bride. "It was those little defects that kept me from getting a better husband."

Being attractive or thin is not enough today; now we must be lean and have muscle definition and endurance. The health clubs tell us we must have hard bodies. Hundreds of thousands of Americans are having parts of their bodies cut, vacuumed, lifted, sanded, implanted, creamed, filled, tweezed, plucked, straightened, waxed, nipped, peeled, and tucked. Many have done this in their relentless battle for perfection and a sense of self-esteem. People are willing to repeatedly risk surgery to have themselves sculpted into their ideal image. I was amazed to hear of a new trend in high school graduation gifts for young women—liposuction. And to think that all I got was luggage!

Dr. Arthur T. Barsky, associate professor of psychiatry at Harvard, explains, "There isn't a surgical solution to unhappiness. We're telling people that unhappiness is medically treatable. When they discover it's not, they feel truly disillusioned and dismayed."[4]

Now, don't get me wrong. I am definitely not against plastic surgery. Heaven knows I've tried to avoid it by standing on my head, hoping everything would fall up! They've told me that what isn't glued on will one day be dropping, drooping, sagging, and bagging. But if this is all we're doing in a search for happiness or self-worth, we won't accomplish it, even with the best surgeon.

Marion Woodman, a psychologist and author of *Addiction to Perfection*, believes, "Women are trying to make their bodies as perfect as possible in compensation for an emptiness inside. They do not see their own beauty. All they see is what is not there. These women," states Woodman, "have to recognize that concentration on the outside is just not going to work."[5] But let's face it, given the choice of having beauty or brains, the vast majority of women would choose beauty. You know why? Because we know that the average man can see better than he can think!

## WHAT ARE YOU DEPENDING UPON?

What are you depending upon for your self-worth? Maybe it depends on how much someone needs you.

Perhaps it's your children. What happens to your self-worth when they no longer need you, when they grow up and leave you, or when they rebel against every good and noble thing you ever taught them?

Maybe it's your spouse. But then what happens if he decides to leave you for another, publicly embarrasses you in some way, is disabled, or dies?

It could even be your career. What happens when they phase out your position in the marketplace or replace you with a computer or someone sharper, younger, more aggressive, and more talented than you? Then what happens to your sense of self-worth?

Maybe your sense of self-worth comes from your net worth. Money can make you feel pretty good about yourself. But let's take a look at what power money really does have. Money can buy a house, but it can't make a happy home. Money can buy medicine, but not good health; a mountain cabin, but not peace of mind when you get there. Money can finance a wonderful wedding, but it can't make a good marriage. Money can buy books, but not wisdom; position, but not honor; acquaintances, but not friends. Money can make you beautiful on the outside, but never on the inside. By what standards are you determining your worth? Perhaps you thought that given enough money, you'd buy yourself happiness, honor, peace, and self-esteem. But it proved to be a cracked vessel of promise that leaked all of your hope.

Maybe your sense of worth is dependent upon what others think of you. The philosopher Marcus Aurelius once said, "I have often wondered how it is that every man sets less value on his own opinion of himself than on the opinion of others. So much more respect have we to what our neighbors think of us than to what we think of ourselves."

For example, the role of mother and housewife was once a high and lofty calling, deserving great respect and honor. Today, this traditional role is being challenged from every direction. It's often considered an inferior role and has become a matter of ridicule in many circles. The opinion of many is that there must be something terribly wrong with the woman who stays at home and likes it!

Read this letter written to Ann Landers, signed "Just a Housewife." Here is her job description:

I am a wife, mother, friend, confidante, personal adviser, lover, referee, peacemaker, housekeeper, laundress, chauffeur, interior decorator, gardener, painter, wallpaperer, dog groomer, veterinarian, manicurist, barber, seamstress, appointment manager, financial planner, bookkeeper, money manager, personal secretary, teacher, disciplinarian, entertainer, psychoanalyst, nurse, diagnostician, public relations expert, dietitian and nutritionist, baker, chef, fashion coordinator and letter writer for both sides of the family.

I am also a travel agent, speech therapist, plumber, automobile maintenance and repair expert. During the course of my day I am supposed to be cheerful, look radiant and jump in the sack on a moment's notice!

From studies done, it would cost over $75,000 (more like $100,00 today) a year to replace me. Do you still feel like just a housewife?[6]

And what about those of you who are single, divorced, or otherwise unmarried? Have you experienced subtle put-downs because of your marital status? It can be very difficult for a woman alone trying to make it in a world seemingly filled with married couples. Some of you have felt like absolute failures. I was there; I know the feeling.

Today we are supposed to look like Miss America, have the energy of Jane Fonda, grasp world events like Barbara Walters, be as versatile as Meryl Streep and as compassionate as Mother Teresa. No wonder we have problems with self-esteem!

By whose standards are you measuring yourself? What identities are you dealing with? We're going to look more closely at the labels, names, and identities that others have given us and those we have given ourselves, and how they have affected us. And we're going to tell ourselves the truth about who we are, the truth of how God sees us.

## LOVE NOTE TO GOD

Lord, I have relied on so many things and people for my self-worth. So often I have failed to consider how You think of me. Help me to see that You value me just as I am, with my failings, my weaknesses, my frustrations, and my strengths. Please give me a greater understanding of the potential You have placed in me. Thank You for the gifts and talents You have given me, and for the love You have lavished upon me.

Love,
Me

## TELLING YOURSELF THE TRUTH

1. What are some of the things or people (other than God) that you depend on for your self-worth or identity?

2. Living up to certain standards is a source of self-esteem. We feel good about ourselves when we meet them, but some are unrealistic. What personal standards have you set up for yourself that you have found to be unrealistic?

Examples:
I must always have a spotless house.
I try to please everyone in my life.
I'll never eat another Mrs. Field's cookie as long as I live.

3. What damages your self-esteem more than anything? How could you change that?

4. If you had no risk of failure, what would you do to make a difference in the world? If you could be anyone in the world, who would you be? Why?

5. If you could change anything in your life, what would it be? Is it possible to begin the steps to change it today?

Examples:
If only I had finished college.
If only I had different parents.
If only I had waited to get married.
If only I had been born rich instead of beautiful.

6. "O LORD, Thou hast searched me and known me. Thou dost know when I sit down and when I rise up;

Thou dost understand my thought from afar. Thou dost scrutinize my path and my lying down, and art intimately acquainted with all my ways. Even before there is a word on my tongue, behold, O LORD, Thou dost know it all. Thou hast enclosed me behind and before, and laid Thy hand upon me. Such knowledge is too wonderful for me; it is too high, I cannot attain to it" (Psalm 139:1-6).

What does God specifically know about you? How does that knowledge make you feel about God? About yourself?

7. "Where can I go from Thy Spirit? Or where can I flee from Thy presence? If I ascend to heaven, Thou art there; If I make my bed in Sheol, behold, Thou art there" (Psalm 139:7-8).

The psalmist marvels at God's knowledge of him, yet in Psalm 139:7-8 he speaks of fleeing from God's presence. Why would he consider this? Does this kind of knowledge give you comfort and peace? Or do you find it embarrassing?

8. "For Thou didst form my inward parts; Thou didst weave me in my mother's womb. I will give thanks to Thee, for I am fearfully and wonderfully made; wonderful are Thy works, and my soul knows it very well. My frame was not hidden from Thee, when I was made in secret, and skillfully wrought in the depths of the earth. Thine eyes have seen my unformed substance; and in Thy book they were all written, the days that were ordained for me, when as yet there was not one of them" (Psalm 139:13-16).

How do you feel about your physical body? How did the psalmist feel? How do you think God feels?

What does it mean to you that God has numbered or ordained all your days?

9. "'For I know the plans that I have for you,' declares the LORD, 'plans for welfare and not for calamity to give you a future and a hope'" (Jeremiah 29:11).

To what extent is God concerned about you? Did you ever experience God's concern for you? When?

10. If God were *lovingly* describing you to one of His angels, what good things might He say about you personally?

# 3

---

# BRAND NAMES

$W$hat's in a name? How about these real names for starters: Viola Unstrung, Daily Swindle, Warren Peace, Blanche Almond, Solomon Gemorah, Pete Moss, Ima June Bug, Ima Hogg, and Fritzi Snickle. To say nothing of Art Gallery, Al Fresca, and Holland Tunnell.

A name gives you something to live up to. Ask a C. Sharpe Minor (organist), U.S. Navey (of the U.S. Marine Corps), Sir Ronaly Brain (neurophysiologist), Zoltan Ovary (gynecologist), or Dick Tracy of Corning, California (police chief). Then there was Charles the Bold, Charles the Handsome, Charles the Idiot (not all the same man), Sancho the Cruel, Ivan the Terrible, and Erik Pinchpenny. Or, what about Paige Turner, Mary Christmas, and the Wind family's children— North, South, East, and West?

The secretary-general of the Organization of American States in 1979 had this to say about his name: "Galo is my Christian name; Plaza is my father's family name; Lasso is my mother's family name. Some call me Mr. Plaza, others Mr. Lasso. In fact, while I was ambassador for Ecuador in the

United Nations, I was called Ambassador Plaza, and people thought I was a hotel."[1]

The Bible tells us that one of the first acts of Adam was naming the animals. After God created woman, Adam named her Eve, which means "the mother of all the living." (You know, of course, that after God created man, He said, "I can do better than that." Then He "fashioned" woman.)

Names in biblical times held significant meanings. For example, Moses' name in Hebrew means "drawn out." His name describes the unique circumstances in which he was found by Pharaoh's daughter. "She named him Moses and said, 'Because I drew him out of the water'" (Exodus 2:10b). Moses' name was a constant reminder to him of who he was and where he had come from.

Names are powerful tools that can dramatically change an individual from one who feels ineffective, inadequate, and incompetent to one who is purposeful, powerful, and productive. You can use these tools to redefine your self-image, to develop a healthy sense of self-esteem, and to realize your true self-worth. And you can apply these powerful tools to the lives of your children, spouse, friends, and significant others to help them understand and better fulfill their God-given potential.

The American painter Charles Willson Peale (1741-1827) had a destiny in mind for his children when he named them. Their names gave them an identity to live up to. There was Rembrandt Peale, Rubens Peale, Raphaelle Peale, and Titian Peale, and they all enjoyed some fame as artists.

Names often denote character qualities that inspire us to live up to them or down to them. As a young boy, Clay overheard his uncle speaking to his father about young Clay's name. "I don't know why you named that boy *Clayton*. Clay is dirt, and that's what his name means—dirt. He'll never amount to anything." "You could be right," the father replied.

How do you think Clay felt about his name after that conversation? He hated it and himself. Who can say how many times a day he heard his name and was reminded of its meaning? Clay began to live up to his name. "For as he thinketh in his heart, so is he" (Proverbs 23:7, KJV). He thought of himself as dirt and considered himself worthless.

Later in his adult life he contacted Midwest Challenge, a rehabilitation program for drug addicts. There he discovered an entirely different way of looking at clay. Clay is a very important raw material when placed in the potter's hand. It is a thing of usefulness, uniqueness, beauty, and value. Clayton learned that God had a plan for his life, that he was indeed important, valuable, useful, and unique. He became a new person. He began to *tell himself the truth.*[2]

## HOMEMADE NAMES

Our names play an important role in our sense of self-worth, which we began to determine by gazing into the mirrors of our parents' eyes. Let me explain. Have you ever been to a hall of mirrors at a fair or circus? All of the mirrors are distorted in some way. Some make us look seven feet tall and thin as a yardstick, with a body that moves like spaghetti. In other mirrors we are stubby, stocky, and short, like a three-foot fireplug. On the way out, the very last mirror brings us back to reality. This last mirror gives us a true, clear, undistorted reflection of ourselves.

Many of us have determined our self-worth by gazing into mirrors that have given us a distorted image of ourselves. Our very early experiences of identity and self-worth come from home—our family, our parents, or those who raised us. The eyes of our parents reflected to us who we were, if we mattered, and how we mattered.

Our parents gave us our first identity, perhaps with comments like "You're so smart." "Just look at how clever and creative you are." "You're going to be the world's best pitcher." "One day you'll be in the big leagues." "Why, you're the most lovable little child that God ever made." "Smart," "clever," "creative," "athletic," and "lovable" were homemade names that carried acceptance, motivation, and encouragement.

My son, Richard Christopher, wrote a paper on his first experiences of identity. His story begins in the cockpit of an airplane.

> At three years old my father let me take the controls of a single engine airplane. I pulled back so far on the steering yoke that the plane began a sharp climb until the angle of ascent was so great the engine could not propel the aircraft any higher. The power began to slip quickly as the plane became almost motionless in midair. Sound from the engine stopped altogether, and my stomach floated as the aircraft literally started dropping out of the sky. Pilots call it a controlled stall, but at three years of age I called it fun! It was great! At the top of those stalls you could hear the wind rush by! My mother called me "adventurer."
>
> Because of my love of flying, I wanted my mother to purchase me a toy airplane, but

instead I remember her saying, "R.C. you can make your own." She said that as though it were as easy as watching television. I now believe that my mother knew exactly what she was doing. She was planting in me the seeds of motivation, creativity, and a desire to realize dreams. Of course the disappointment of not having the store-bought toy remained for a while, but I soon employed some ingenuity. I began creating airplanes out of various household items—cooking utensils, bobby pins, and pencils. She consistently told me that I was able to meet a challenge, create something, or solve a problem. Never being told you have limitations is really a wonderful thing. She reinforced my identity when she made me feel pride in my "creations." My identity became "creative."

It was when I developed an obsession for architecture that I began to realize there was something different about me. By the time I was fourteen years old I was designing homes and actually had them built! Over twenty buildings are still standing as a testimony to the fact. With my picture in the newspaper and some keenly interested school teachers surrounding me, I was labeled "gifted." I have since been immersed in philosophy, rhetoric, politics, and music. I've written minor symphonies, taken up a variety of instruments, and have created over a hundred pieces of jazz to my name. However, I can clearly recall telling people, "What's the big deal; anybody could do it." Believing that almost anything was possible had become as easy as watching television and as much fun as hearing the wind rush by. I thought everyone had my mother for a parent.

(Of course I paid my young son handsomely for his comments.) R.C. is presently at the University of Montana studying political science with a goal of entering politics. Move over, Mr. President. We're changing the drapes in the oval office.

## "THE ONE WITH MOXIE"

When some of you looked into the mirrors of your parents' eyes, you knew they were crazy about you. Even if they never said it, you just knew they thought you were terrific, they believed in you, and you mattered to them. You began to live up to their image of you.

Living up to the expectations of others could be a definition of John Politan's life. John, a dynamic attorney, is the grandson of an Italian immigrant family. John had an uncle named Tony who was always considered to be "the one with moxie." Tony was made a local celebrity overnight when he won four-years' paid tuition at Illinois Normal Teacher's College. Uncle Tony became the rallying point for the Italian-American community in that part of the state. They felt he would someday be a lawyer and a spokesman for their interests. But just a few days before his college classes began, Tony's life was cut short by a shooting incident.

It was an enormous loss to everyone and had far-reaching effects. Young John was only four years old when he first remembers hearing his father say, "John, you're the next Tony," and all the relatives would nod in agreement. Through the years, his father repeated this over and over again to John, especially when another family member or friend was around so they could chime in and agree with him. John was frequently told "You have Tony's brains," and "Here's the one who will fulfill the dream of college and law school for the family." From the earliest moment of his life, John was instilled with a sense of purpose and destiny: to be a lawyer and realize the family dream. When he was still quite young, he was drawn to any TV programs, movies, and books that dealt with lawyers and courtroom dramas. He was so motivated by his family's belief in his abilities that he even went so far as to memorize and practice lines of dialogue from *Inherit the Wind*. John said, "I stood in front of a mirror and practiced their gestures, the way they stood at the jury box, how they handled the cross-examination, and how they gave their jury summations." His sense of purpose and destiny shaped everything he did from an intellectual and educational standpoint.

Two final points should be made about this. First, John was not "pushed" into becoming a lawyer. John said, "It wasn't like my parents were 'stage mothers' who were trying to live out their fantasies through my life. It was their verbal expression of what they envisioned as my future destiny that took hold of me and had this impact on my life." What a picture of the influence and impact others' images can have on us! Secondly, John acknowledges, "I have certain natural gifts and abilities which all of the books and training over the years simply refined and sharpened. None of it would have been allowed to happen if it were not God's ultimate plan for my life."

## NAMES OF REJECTION

Maybe "lovable," "lawyer," "talented," and "the one with moxie" don't sound like what you heard at home. You were given names all right, but they were painful reminders of the constant rejection you experienced—names like "You're so stupid. Can't you ever do anything right?" "Just look at how clumsy you are—always dropping things." "You'll never graduate from high school, considering how lazy you are." "No, you can't have any cookies; you're already too fat." "You're hopeless." "Homemade" names.

Some of you saw rejection in the eyes of your parents. They didn't even have to say it; you knew. "You won't ever amount to anything. You're just a loser and an inconvenience. Let's face it, you just don't measure up. You don't matter to us or to anyone." They communicated to you that you would never meet their expectations. We tend to live up to the expectations others have of us, don't we? Positive and negative.

A few of you heard "You'll never amount to anything," and you said, "Oh yeah, I'll show them." You determined to become a perfectionist, an overachiever, and at fifty years of age you're still "showing them."

Diana at age forty-eight defines herself as a perfectionist who grew up in a family where she was continually trying to prove her worth. Diana's mother was terribly embarrassed when at age forty-two she became pregnant with Diana. In those days many women did not consider pregnancy at that age as something to hope for or be proud of. Her mother tried to hide the fact until hiding was no longer a possibility.

Diana recalls shopping with her gray-haired mother and people often asking, "Is this your granddaughter?" To which her mother would reply, "Why yes." To Diana it was rejection.

As far back as Diana can remember, her father never called her by her given name. He always called her "Runt." She thought perhaps he gave her that name because she was petite and the last of the "litter of six" children. But Diana's parents did not discern her temperament or personality. Nor was attention paid as to how all this affected her self-image. Diana hated to be teased and felt it terribly degrading to be called "Runt." But she heard it over and over again all through her childhood. She used to think, "Runt of the litter. That's me." That was her identity.

Diana's mother was a perfectionist in her appearance and in her housekeeping. No matter what Diana did she was never quite perfect enough to receive any recognition. The message communicated to her was "You'll never really amount to anything," despite the fact that Diana was a superb student and excelled at playing the piano in competition. Inside of that tender little girl was a heart desiring to please and to be noticed. She worked diligently at whatever task was before her and felt she had to be perfect at it. She thought if she could do it perfectly, then maybe they would recognize her for it. It never happened, but striving for perfection became a way of life. It was a way of trying to earn a word of praise, approval, or encouragement for the little girl named "Runt."

Through her relationship with Jesus Christ and her loving, supportive, husband, Jay, Diana has been able to deal with the wounds of her childhood. Today she is a beautiful, still wonderfully petite, mother of four who has raised her children with a strong, healthy sense of self-esteem.

## AS YOU THINK IN YOUR HEART, SO YOU ARE

None of us had perfect parents. They were human, sometimes having poor judgment, giving unwise counsel, being manipulative or overly critical, or unable to express love or praise. They were, just as we are, less than perfect. Some of us experienced negative input.

If affirmation, acceptance, and love were not given to us as children, then we came to the only conclusion we could—we must not be of much value. If they communicated to us that we were natural-born winners or natural-born losers, how did we know any different?

Norman Vincent Peale tells a story that illustrates this principle very well. While walking through the streets of Kowloon in Hong Kong, Dr. Peale came upon a tattoo studio. In the window the artist displayed many sample tattoos. You could have just about anything tattooed on yourself—a large heart with *Mother* on it, an anchor, the American flag. But there was one tattoo that seemed strange for anyone to put permanently on his flesh. It was the phrase *Born to Lose*. Some people may have *Born to Win* or maybe even *Born to Shop*, but *Born to Lose?* When the tattoo artist was questioned as to whether anyone ever had that terrible phrase tattooed on his body, he answered, "Yes, sometimes." But then the Chinese artist tapped his forehead and said, "Before tattoo on body, tattoo on mind."[3] Friends, "As a man thinks in his heart, so is he."

What about nicknames or pet names? Have you ever given your children pet names? I called mine "mon petit chou," which actually means "my little cabbage head." It was probably a good thing they couldn't speak French. I could have damaged them permanently. "Hey Richard and Shannon, what did your parents call you as kids?" "Vegetables. How about you?" I couldn't go to my grave knowing that I'd done that to my children. For all of you who fear irreparable harm has been done to my babies, trust me; it's okay. They know it was a term of endearment and they love it. They're still "my little cabbage heads," but at twenty-nine and thirty years of age, I have to be a bit discerning about using the term. I don't leave it on their answering machines.

Did your parents have a pet name, or nickname, for you? Maybe you were called Dumbo, Stinky, Jug Ears (which resurfaced as a nickname after the 1992 presidential elections), Curly, Pee Wee, Fatso, or Lumpy. Perhaps it was Princess, Twiggy, or Miss Piggy, Peaches, Pumpkin, or Petunia. We loved them or hated them, but they left their mark.

As children we began to think in our hearts and live out who we thought we were. The tender identity of our self-worth was forming. Many of the labels of our childhood were "homemade," some created by very loving hands, some by hands not so loving. Yes, it's true, our life was greatly shaped by the environment and manner in which we were raised. But aren't you just a little tired of people saying they came from a dysfunctional family? "My sister looked at me cross-eyed, and I haven't been right since!" "My mother wouldn't give me a second helping of apple pie, and now I just can't seem to relate to women." Do you know anyone who came from a perfectly normal family where everyone did everything right? Where there were no hurt feelings, no misunderstandings, and no imperfect people? Healing will begin as we gain insight into how we got to be the way we are, not as we focus on placing blame.

## I DISCOVERED THE "LIE"

"Sticks and stones may break my bones, but names will never hurt me." I used to believe that with my whole heart and even sang it to the big kids who taunted me when I was in kindergarten. But in fourth grade I discovered it was a lie.

As we were studying geography, my teacher asked if anyone had ancestors from Czechoslovakia. I was so proud to raise my hand, because I was the only one. I was in a class by myself! Oh to be so wonderfully distinctive. Not only did I have ancestors from Czechoslovakia, but both my parents were Slovak. Was I unique or what?

I stood with unfaltering pride, ready to receive the accolades and applause for having been born into such a heritage. Without warning, my teacher's words broke my euphoria. "Well then, Roberta, you're a Slav." "A what?" A brick to my forehead would have been more welcomed than that comment. What we as fourth graders heard was "Roberta, you're a slob." They repeated it, they giggled, they howled, and they ridiculed me. They sang it till I could bear it no more, "Roberta is a slob, Roberta is a slob." I was devastated, and humiliated. By the time the teacher gained control, it was too late. I hated them, myself, and my teacher. I was angry at every ancestor I'd ever had.

For years after that episode I was embarrassed about my heritage. To my surprise, this memory surfaced just a year ago as I was working on this book. And for the first time I understood why I felt the way I did. (We're talking a lot of years here.) Immediately I knew I had to forgive my classmates and that teacher, whose name I still remember.

## BRAND NAMES

As we grew up, others continued to give us mirrored reflections of ourselves as they saw us. Some positive, some negative, but often inaccurate. Our teachers, friends, coaches, peers, employers, and other significant people in our lives "branded" us as they saw us perform in the arena of life—"brand names."

Names and identities based on social status, appearance, family name, wealth, education, or performance were given to us. Labels like "enthusiastic," "fun loving," "party girl," "bookworm," "jock," "hard driver," "pothead," "drugger," "ne'er-do-well," "valedictorian," "beauty queen," "salesperson-of-the-year," "mother-of-the-year," "career woman," "divorced," and so on. By now our estimation of ourselves was becoming rather firmly fixed in our minds. What is your estimation of yourself? How do you perceive yourself? Is it the truth? How can you really know the truth about yourself? Stay tuned. The answers are coming.

God filled us with the capacity for greatness, yet some of us listened to the negative attitudes of others. We bought into the lie and allowed other people's words to rob us of the potential that God had for us. I heard someone once say, "What other people think of you is none of your business." We need to think, believe, and tell the truth about ourselves—from God's perspective. We need to see the people God sees.

## SEEING THE POTENTIAL IN ANOTHER

There may have been a few special people who crossed your path, who truly cared about you and believed in you. Maybe there was only one. Sometimes that's all it takes. Think of that one person who influenced your life in a very positive way—someone who saw potential in you, encouraged you, and believed in you.

You saw in that person's eyes a reflection of not only who you were but who you could become. That individual was willing to pay a price for you by investing energy, time, and love into you. Before this week is out, write a note or, if possible, tell that person what he or she has meant to you. Give that person the encouragement we all need to hear: "You are valued; you made a great difference in my life. You made me see myself as a person of worth. You pointed me in the right direction. You caused me to see that I was valuable. You gave me hope. Thank you, dear friend."

Have you ever been that "important person" to someone else? Is there an individual in your life who desperately needs to hear words of affirmation and acceptance? Be that person of encouragement to another.

There is a special woman who stands out in my mind as one of my top cheerleaders, encouragers, and motivators. Terry Fenwick saw me as having far more potential than I ever thought possible. She has an infectious personality and touches all who cross her path with her enthusiasm and zest for living. It all springs from her love of the Lord which she freely shares. She believed in what the Lord could do through me if I were willing and yielded. Terry communicated this to me in a hundred different ways.

She was the first one who ever challenged me to get up in front of an audience and speak. She said, "Roberta, you've got the gift of teaching. Now develop it." Terry and our mutual friend Anne Anderson provided opportunities for me to speak that I would never have had otherwise. I had to stretch and grow to meet the call. Thank you, dear friends; you are valued.

How good of the Lord to send people into our lives to inspire and motivate us to greatness. The manager of the Chicago Cubs, Jimmy Lefevbre, was a former all-star infielder for the L.A. Dodgers. He was also the 1965 National League rookie of the year. Jimmy related his experience in encouragement to me. When Jimmy was five years old, his father told him, "Jimmy, someday you're going to play in the big leagues." Jimmy lived in Inglewood, California, at the time. His childhood was made up of food and baseballs, school and baseball gloves, sleep and baseball bats, and more baseball. The Lefevbre's backyard became Yankee Stadium every afternoon. Jimmy, his twin brother, and all their friends played "in the big leagues" throughout their childhood.

Jimmy said, "When we called out, 'play ball,' that backyard ballpark became our stadium. As I grew up, the game of baseball never changed, only the stadiums." The day came when Jimmy found himself playing at Yankee Stadium in the World Series. Jimmy said, "I started to get into the batter's box, and then I stepped back out. I looked up at the fans, the stadium, the opposing players, and I thought to myself, I'm supposed to be here. I've been here before. I've practiced for this all my life. It's like another rehearsal." "Someday, Jimmy, you're going to be in the big leagues."

Because someone saw great potential in him, believed in him, and encouraged him, Jimmy believed what he was told. Yes, he had talent. Yes, he was intense. And, yes, he had desire. He also was given an identity that he intended to live up to, and he did.

Parents, grandparents, teachers, and friends have an extraordinary opportunity here to positively affect the lives of others. There are chances to influence and enhance the lives of all we come in contact with, but especially the "little people"—the children for whom we have been given responsibility from God to encourage, motivate, inspire, and affirm. Enkindle within them a fire to fulfill their God-given potential. Teach them how to see themselves from God's perspective—as children of value and worth.

We have such a small window of time when they are young, open, and eager to believe the "impossible" for themselves. That season of their lives passes quickly, and soon the world tells them "It can't be done." And some of those young minds believe it. History is filled with the "It can't be done people":

"Everything that can be invented has been invented." Charles H. Duell, Director of U.S. Patent Office, 1899

"There is no likelihood man can ever tap the power of the atom." Robert Millikan, Nobel Prize in Physics, 1920

"Heavier than air flying machines are impossible." Lord Kelvin, President, Royal Society, c.1895

"Sensible and responsible women do not want to vote." Grover Cleveland, 1905

Are there some names and identities that have cracked the tender places of your life? Perhaps your memories are full of anguish and bitterness. I cannot change your past; it is gone, though you bear the scars. I cannot change those who are hurting you today, but I can do one important thing. I can give you hope for all your tomorrows. I can point you to the One who is the source of all our hope—Jesus Christ. Jesus determined how much we are valued by giving His life for us. He is the key to our opinion of ourselves.

So the mother with her hands on her hips stands before the child and impatiently rebukes him, "Who do you think you are?" The child in all innocence replies, "I don't know. Who do I think I am?" So is the child in us all, looking for the answer to our identity and self-worth. The ultimate source of self-esteem is found only in a relationship with our Perfect Parent, the Master Designer himself.

## LOVE NOTE TO GOD

Dear Lord, I come to You in weakness to ask for Your strength. I come to You in need of wisdom, for I have been so foolish. I come to You for truth, for I have been deceived. I come to You in search of my true worth and identity. Please reveal Yourself to me, that I might know You, the Living God, the answer to all of my needs. Oh Lord, I have so many hurting, broken places. I bring them to You to lay at Your feet. Please take my burdens; they are far too heavy for my shoulders; my wounds are still so fresh. Heal my broken places. Thank you, dear Lord, for Your tender mercies.

Love,
Me

## TELLING YOURSELF THE TRUTH

1. List some of the positive "brand names" that you were given. What difference have they made in your sense of self-worth? What were some of the negative labels and identities that you were given by others? How did they affect you? Did you decide to believe them? Why?

2. List three ways you could demonstrate to someone that he or she is a person of worth and value. Has anyone ever done this for you? What was your reaction?

3. Have you ever failed to try something because of low self-esteem? What were the results? How would you do it differently today?

4. List three pleasing character qualities you possess. Which ones were encouraged at home?

5. Imagine yourself being your parent and raising you. What would you do differently than your own parents? How would you treat yourself? How would you speak to yourself?

6. Do you know what your name means? (You might want to look it up in *What's in a Name?*) If you don't know, what character quality does it seem to convey to you—strength, nobility, grace, beauty,

wisdom, joy? Do you live up to it? What character qualities do you think God wants you to live up to?

7. When we rely solely on the opinions of other people for our self-worth, what happens to our identity? What happens if their opinions change?

"For I, the LORD, do not change" (Malachi 3:6). How does God change? Does God change His opinion of you?

8. "'For I know the plans that I have for you,' declares the LORD, 'plans for welfare and not for calamity to give you a future and a hope. Then you will call upon Me and come and pray to Me, and I will listen to you. And you will seek Me and find Me, when you search for Me with all your heart. And I will be found by you,' declares the LORD" (Jeremiah 29:11-14).

If someone rejects you, what is your response? Do you think God rejects anyone who comes to Him?

9. "But we all, with unveiled face beholding as in a mirror the glory of the Lord, are being transformed into the same image from glory to glory, just as from the Lord, the Spirit" (2 Corinthians 3:18).

What is the One undistorted mirror in which we can see our true image? What are we being transformed into? How does the knowledge of that fact make you feel?

10. "And do not be conformed to this world, but be transformed by the renewing of your mind, that you

may prove what the will of God is, that which is good and acceptable and perfect" (Romans 12:2).

How can we be transformed by the renewing of our mind? Do you imagine it might mean to think the truth? What can we fill our minds with in order to tell ourselves the truth and be transformed?

# 4

## THE DESIGNER'S CREATION

About twenty-five years ago, I was taking flying lessons. My husband, Robert, says, "Roberta as a pilot, now there is a frightening thought. At least when she is driving, we can stay out of the streets. With her in the air this planet isn't safe!" I'm honestly not offended by his comment. There is more than a grain of truth in it.

It was in my ground school class that I began to learn a very important lesson: Emotions or feelings are not to be completely trusted. A pilot must learn to trust the instruments in the cockpit, and not fly on feelings. Do you remember the movie *Top Gun*? The aerial dogfights in the F-16s were sensational. The planes were all over the sky, upside down, right side up, and even sideways. The problem is that the airplane can be upside down, but the pilot may feel he's right side up. There is an instrument in the cockpit called the attitude indicator, whereby one can determine where the aircraft is in relation to the horizon. The pilot is taught to trust his instruments, not his feelings or the seat of his pants.

I took up flying in Los Angeles, where sudden fog banks are a common occurrence. Within minutes you can be in total fog with zero visibility. Let's say you and I went out flying and we got caught in a fog bank. How confident would you be if I said, "Well, you know I just don't believe those instruments. I have a feeling the airport is probably over there. What do you think? Gee, it's foggy. I can't see a thing out there, can you?" You'd be searching for a parachute, calling the tower, and wisely making your peace with God.

Feelings don't always give us a true reading on situations. When a friend or relative has just hurt our feelings, we're sure nobody likes us, and our self-esteem is in the pits. You go shopping for your high school reunion, and the sales clerk remarks, "Let's try the next size up. It's sure to be more flattering." Your best friend is introducing you, and she forgets your name. You come home after a hard day expecting to be welcomed by faithful Fido, and he's left a farewell note. When our world seems upside down, emotions can't always be trusted.

Well, then, how can we get a true reading on ourselves? What do we use for our "attitude indicator"? We don't come equipped with cockpit instruments that automatically provide an accurate reading, but there is a place we can go for the truth about who we are. There is the highest authority, an opinion that is totally trustworthy: the Bible, the inerrant, inspired Word of God. "All Scripture is inspired by God and profitable for teaching, for reproof, for correction, for training in righteousness" (2 Timothy 3:16).

## YOU'RE NO CHICKEN!

Knowing the truth about your identity can make all the difference in the world. A story is told of a rancher who lived in the Southwest. After hunting one day, he came upon an injured baby eagle. He scooped up that eaglet and took him back to the ranch. The chicken yard seemed like the best place to put him, and so there he stayed and there he grew. Before long this little eagle was getting along famously with all the chickens. He was scratching in the dirt, strutting around, and even trying to make "chicken noises." (You hang around with the chickens long enough, you start thinking like one.) Nobody told him he was an eagle and that he could fly.

One day the rancher's friend stopped by and commented on the magnificent eagle grubbing around in the dirt with all those chickens. "Friend, that eagle was designed to soar on the clouds. He needs to discover his potential and his wings." "Naw," replied the rancher, "he doesn't know any better. Look at him. He thinks he's a chicken. He'll never fly."

The friend was insistent as he climbed a fence with the eagle under his arm. It wasn't a very high fence, but he was certain that with just a little help that eagle would ride into the winds. He eagerly lifted him into the air and said, "You are an eagle and you were meant to soar." Then he let him peel off. With a power dive ending in a crash and burn, the eagle made quick contact with the earth. He fell flat on his beak, squawking and complaining like a henhouse full of foxes.

The rancher's friend wasn't going to give up so quickly. He decided to climb a very high cliff with his "chicken-minded" friend in hand. The man stood at the edge of the cliff, felt the blustery wind rush by, and shouted, "You are an eagle and you were meant to soar." At first the eagle didn't have a clue; he flapped, faltered, and fishtailed. Then in one wonderful moment a wind shear picked him up, and he discovered he had wings. He could fly, he could ride the winds, he could soar just as he was designed to do. He discovered his identity.

Maybe no one has told you that you're not a chicken but an eagle. God made you to soar. God created you to enjoy the rarefied air of His presence and power. When you allow God to fill you with His Spirit and His strength, you will no longer be bound by the opinions of others. You were created to depend on the Lord for your identity: "Yet those who wait for the Lord will gain new strength; they will mount up with wings like eagles, they will run and not get tired, they will walk and not become weary" (Isaiah 40:31).

Whom will you choose to believe about your true value? Distorted mirrors, feelings, and emotions, or a clear reflection in the mirror of God's Word, the Bible? I search the Bible to learn what God thinks about me because His thoughts are the truest things about me. The me God sees—that's who I truly am.

In the first chapter of Genesis we read, "Then God said, Let Us make man in Our image, according to Our likeness....And God created man in His own image, in the image of God He created him; male and female He created them." God scooped up a lump of clay from the earth, carefully crafted and formed a man, brought it to his lips, and breathed life into him. The man began to breathe, move, speak, and think. The Creator had put his fingerprint upon that clay. He created man in His image.

## A GAP IN HISTORY

You are indeed a distinctive being. Think about who you are for a moment. What a miraculous thing it is to be you. No one is like you, nor can you be duplicated. No person who has ever lived or ever will live has the exact same personality, character, talents, and abilities that you do. No one has the same physical appearance, will enjoy the same opportunities, or is loved by the same combination of people. No one's hair even grows like yours does. No one has the same birth order in your family as you do. You are absolutely unique. If you had not been born, there would be a gap in history.

The movie *It's a Wonderful Life*, starring Jimmy Stewart and Donna Reed, has become a classic. Jimmy Stewart plays a man named George Bailey who is contemplating suicide by jumping off a bridge. He has fallen into some hard times, and this seems like the answer to him.

Meanwhile, up in heaven God is giving the angel Clarence an assignment to rescue George. Clarence is trying to earn his wings, so he is quite willing to do whatever it takes. Clarence takes on the form of a man, beats George to the punch, and jumps into the water first. Clarence calls for help while thrashing around in the river. George, being the big-hearted guy that he is, rescues Clarence from a watery grave instead of ending his own life.

When George tells him how miserable he is and how he wishes he had never been born, Clarence gets a brilliant idea and shows George what life would be like if he had never been born. George saved his brother's life as a young boy. He protected a pharmacist from accidentally filling a prescription with a poisonous drug. He helped a young woman to seek a better life. His mother would have been a poor lonely widow. His wife, Mary, would never have married, and on and on. Clarence says, "George, there would be an incredible gap in history had you never been born." And it was true.

You have a place in life that only you can fill. There is no substitute for you, and there is no person that can replace you. You are a custom-designed, handmade original. You are one of a kind!

## MASTERPIECE OF GOD'S CREATION

Did you know you are the masterpiece of God's creation? This is your identity! And these bodies, are they not remarkably designed?

Six-year-old Ian volunteered to say grace before dinner one evening. He seemed very pleased to thank God for the great food he was about to eat and the fun activities of his day. Then he paused and said, "And thank You, God, for the nice little boy You gave this family." His mother gasped, "Nice little boy? Where?" "Right here," he grinned, pointing to himself. "I was thanking God for me." Ian was confident of his identity. As his mother was washing the dishes that evening, it occurred to her that her son had a point. Ian understood he was "individually crafted with the compliments of His Creator" and just wanted to thank Him. Immediately she was overwhelmed as she realized she had never thanked God for creating her. As she stood at the sink, elbow deep in soapsuds, she quietly prayed, "Thank You, God, for all the workmanship You put into making me."[1]

Stop right now. Think of some part of your body that you are really grateful for—creative hands, great head of hair, strong legs, good eyes, or a quick mind— because these are parts of a wonderful masterpiece. Thank God for how He made you. We are God's masterpiece because God choose to dwell in human form when Jesus Christ took on flesh and walked upon this earth.

## WHAT ONE IS WILLING TO PAY DETERMINES THE VALUE

The value of something is the price one is willing to pay. Wouldn't you agree? What is a free loaf of bread worth to a man who has just eaten three quarter pounders, one taco supreme, two packages of fries, and one large malt? He'd trade that loaf of bread for a package of Rolaids any day. However, to a starving man this same loaf of bread is worth life itself. He'd give anything to have it.

Several years ago a painting entitled *Irises* by Vincent van Gogh sold for $53.9 million. Now the canvas and paint were barely worth $10 by today's standards, yet Alan Bond, an Australian financier, was willing to pay an incredible price for this work of art.

At another auction Pablo Picasso's *Acrobat and Young Harlequin* was bought for $38.46 million. It was purchased by a Japanese buyer who became quite emotional over the acquisition. I would be too, but probably not for the same reason. The buyer was so excited to have this wonderful masterpiece that he didn't even question the price.

Would you think any differently of yourself if someone very famous and important regarded you as a treasure of inestimable value, like a great work of art, a masterpiece? That is the you God sees!

Certainly one of the reasons that the paintings by Picasso and van Gogh were purchased for millions was that each was unique. There is not another one of them in all the world. Your life, even before your birth, was an empty canvas on which God began to paint a masterpiece. He picked up His palette of stained-glass window colors and painted shapes, shades, and sizes in a way that He had never done before. And God made you. He never mass-produces copies. Each is distinctively different.

The two art collectors willingly paid an enormous price for each unique masterpiece. Jesus Christ did the same for you and for every other unique masterpiece in the world. Do not forget that "you are not your own. For you have been bought with a price" (1 Corinthians 6:19-20).

## YOU'RE ONE IN FIVE MILLION

You are no accident of nature. You did not happen by chance. Scripture says that God has known you since before the foundation of the world. Your birth was no mistake, and you were definitely no surprise to God. Read what King David wrote: "My frame was not hidden from Thee, when I was made in secret, and skillfully wrought in the depths of the earth. Thine eyes have seen my unformed substance; and in Thy book they were all written, the days that were ordained for me, when as yet there was not one of them" (Psalm 139:15-16).

Did you know that at the time of your conception there were over five million sperm and just one egg? Think of the odds! You are one in five million! You are not an accident of nature. God intended for you to be born.

The humanist believes that we evolved from nothing, by chance, and that our eternal destiny is also nothingness. So unbelieving man rejects God as Creator and falls at the feet of chance and worships there. He will not recognize his need for Jesus Christ nor desire to spend eternity with Him. If his destiny is nothingness, what does he need a savior for? What people believe about how they were created will make a great difference in their identity, self-worth, behavior, attitudes, morals, and values. It will also set the standard for how they treat their own body.

Where did I come from? Who am I? What is my purpose? Where am I going? How can anyone possibly develop a healthy identity if they don't know the answers to these questions? Our fundamental mistake, however, is that we think that the answer begins with us and not with God. We become so introspective, always looking for the answers within ourselves. The truth is that God is the center from which all life comes and takes meaning. We are not the center of all things; God is.

## IMAGE BEARER OF CHRIST

God says that we were created by Him in His image. Well, then, how were we made in His image? We were created in the likeness of God—likeness such as intellect, emotions, will, creativity, and with a spirit. We were created with the capacity to reflect His glory and His character.

I had a wonderful friend from Houston, Texas, who had the most delightful drawl. When I spent a lot of time with Peggy, I'd start talking like her. The most wonderful drawl would develop in the span of a few hours! I even took on some of her unique expressions. That's a small picture of how it is with God. We were meant to live in such a close personal relationship with Jesus Christ that we would take on His character. We were created to be an "Image Bearer" of Jesus Christ. What a privilege! What an awesome responsibility! This is our identity! As a friend of mine once said, "If we hang out with Jesus long enough, we'll start sounding like Him."

Think of it this way. Wherever a pregnant woman goes, everyone recognizes the fact that she is different; she is carrying another life within her. She takes special care of herself, eating the proper foods and getting enough rest. She will often read books about this new life growing in her. She is careful not to put herself in unhealthy circumstances. She is treated differently by others, and it is an unmistakable fact that she carries the presence of a child within her.

We who know Jesus Christ should bear the unmistakable presence of Christ. Look at your life today. Does the world know that you are different? Are you bearing Christ within you? Are you compassionate with the sick, the lonely, the retarded, the elderly? Do you forgive those who have wronged you, lied to you, deceived you, forsaken you, disappointed you? Do you love only those who love you, only those who think the way you do, only those who act the way you want them to? Consider the example that you set in the world. Does the world see the unmistakable presence of God within you? God has bestowed great dignity and honor upon believers. God has created value and worth in us and stamped His Image upon His own. He has put His unique thumbprint on us.

Saint Augustine was an "Image Bearer" of Christ and a great man of God. Before he committed his life to Jesus, he led a wild life of "wine, women, and song." One day while walking along a city street, he spotted a woman who had been his mistress in his years before becoming a Christian. He glanced over at her and felt the old stirring within him. Immediately he crossed the street and ran the opposite way. She called to him, "Augustine, Augustine, it is I." He ran with furor all the faster, crying out loud to himself,

"Augustine, Augustine, dost thou not know that thou art carrying God within thee?"

You, believer-in-Christ, are you aware that you are carrying God within you? The truest thing about you is what God has spoken. The one, the only true mirror that will give you a reflection with zero distortions is in the eyes of our Lord. Our true identity is found in Him, in a personal relationship with Jesus Christ. He offers Himself to us that we might be transformed and bear His signature on our life.

## LOVE NOTE TO GOD

Lord God of mercy, I didn't know that you put such value on me. Forgive me for not being aware of bearing Your image, of carrying You within me, of reflecting Your character and Your glory. I have not always shown the world who You are. I have been unkind, hateful, unforgiving, selfish, greedy, and bitter. This is not Your image; it is my flesh. You have considered me far more highly and with greater worth than I have considered myself. I am humbled by Your graciousness toward me. Teach me how to live my life with the full knowledge that I bear Your signature.

Love,
Me

---

## TELLING YOURSELF THE TRUTH

1. How does the world tell us that we are not valuable?

2. List three things (not counting your children) that would not have happened had you never been born.

3. Do you bear a likeness to your mother and father? How? What likenesses do we share with God?

4. What does the phrase "created in God's image" mean to you? What difference does this make in your identity?

5. "What is man that you are mindful of him, the son of man, that you care for him? You made him a little lower than the heavenly beings and crowned him with glory and honor. You made him ruler over the works of your hands; you put everything under his feet" (Psalm 8:4-6, NIV).

Describe how God views us. What does it mean to you to be crowned "with glory and honor"? How could this knowledge make a practical difference in the way we live? What have we done to earn such honor?

6. Read Genesis 3. In your opinion, why did Adam and Eve disobey? Had God been withholding anything from them?

7. Are you grasping and striving for something with your own hands, thinking that God may be withholding it? Have you ever "helped God out" by meeting your own need to feel more important or for a heightened sense of identity? How?

8. Read Genesis 3:8-19. What do you think Adam and Eve's sense of self-esteem was like after God pronounced His judgments upon them? What might

we conclude about sin and how it affects our self-esteem and identity?

9. Eve was deceived and believed the lie of Satan, the serpent. What lie are you believing about your true self-worth and identity?

10. What would you tell fellow believers who feel they are worthless and hopeless?

# 5

---

# GOD'S WORK OF ART

Shaping pots was one of my favorite activities as an art student. Many an hour was spent "throwing" pots and loving it. My pottery professor gave us an assignment to make our vessels out of the clay we dug from the surrounding foothills of Sacramento. It was a great project, but I had no idea what "living lessons" were wrapped up in a lifeless lump of clay.

First of all, when I brought the clay back to the studio, it had all kinds of debris in it—stones, dead bugs, straw, weeds. And I was supposed to make a lovely pot out of this formless mass of clay filled with impurities. Of course, I had to remove most of the debris, but there were still a few scraps of "stuff" I had to deal with later.

The clay was cleansed, prepared, and ready to be shaped by my hands on the wheel. A little pressure here, a little pulling there, and lots of water to make the clay malleable. It was a wonderfully messy affair. I wore big old shoes, denim overalls, and an enormous smile. You couldn't tell where the clay ended and I began. Finally a vessel began to emerge out of the shapeless lump. Then suddenly a small stone, a tiny bug, or an occasional weed would pop out. They, of course, had to be removed. Several times the pot would be marred in my hands, but I'd form it into another pot as it seemed best to me. A work of art was in process.

## WE ARE GOD'S WORKMANSHIP

When God formed us, He also was creating a work of art. Ephesians 2:10 says, "For we are His workmanship, created in Christ Jesus for good works...." The word *workmanship* in Greek carries the connotation of a "work of art"—"God's work of art." We spend our days working on things that matter to us. God does the same. He is working on us; we are the work of God. God loves us passionately and is creating perfection in us, as a result of His love, grace, and indwelling Presence.

The day we were born we were named, not numbered. We are not just a product of our parents. Who we are and who we will become is in the mind of God. He made us, formed us, and gave us understanding and an identity that no one can refute.

Several months ago a dear young friend of mine, Trisha, discovered she was pregnant. What a joy! Baby showers, baby clothes, and most important, baby's new name. What wonderful news! Only one major problem—Trisha wasn't married. So it was indeed a bittersweet moment as Judy, her mother, shared her burden with me. As for Trisha, she didn't excuse her behavior; she dealt with her sin before God.

But as we know, some sins have greater consequences than others. One day I was hugging this precious young woman, and I said, "Look, your sin is no more sinful than any of ours. It's just that some of our sins are not quite so obvious." Trisha agreed and said, "Right. And in a few months mine is going to be incredibly obvious." Trisha believes in the inestimable significance of life, so she chose to protect this precious baby from those who would tell her it is too inconvenient, undesirable, and untimely.

When Trisha was five months pregnant, she went in for an ultrasound, accompanied by Judy. They haven't been the same since. What they saw was what God has been privileged to witness since the beginning of time—the mystery of a tiny human being growing in the womb. We are now privileged to gaze upon the private chambers of His secret work. As Judy and Trisha watched wide eyed, they saw a one and one-half pound baby that could fit in the palm of their hand. They saw his little turned up nose and could even see his tiny heart beating. And guess what? He was sucking his thumb! He was a complete baby. Judy said, "Roberta, it was the most amazing sight. He was lying on his back with his legs crossed at the knees, as if he were thinking, This life is the berries! I'll just kick back, relax, and enjoy the next meal. He looked as if he didn't have a care in the world. He already has a personality!"

Trisha went through a real transformation at that moment. Until then, she hadn't thought of the baby as a real person, but at that point she became fully aware that a unique human being was developing inside of her. No longer secret, unseen, or unknown. It was the beginning of a delightful love affair with that new baby. She realized that God was creating a work of art within her.

Walking out of the office, Trisha realized how self-centered she had been. Up to that point, she was only thinking about herself, her needs, and her predicament. Now she considers, "What can I do for my child? How can I best take care of the health and welfare of this baby?" Trisha said, "I really don't think about myself as often as I think about this baby." This was a cherished moment for Judy and Trisha as they shared what was once for God's eyes only. Do you think God considers ultrasound a wonderful tool, enabling us to see the Master Designer's new work of art? What a privilege! Surely this would leave every eyewitness with an overwhelming desire to protect this winsome, tiny treasure.

Our little bit of life executes a backflip in the womb and muses, "I think I'll just kick back, suck my thumb, and enjoy this safe place while God's working on me. When He was creating my nose, He said, 'This is just the right shape. I think I'll turn it up a little at the end.' I overheard Him say something about making a 'masterpiece.' I must be a handmade original! And you know what? I remember when He told me He loved me. It was when He gave me my beating heart." The psalmist would agree: "For Thou didst form my inward parts; Thou didst weave me in my mother's womb....My frame was not hidden from Thee, when I was made in secret, and skillfully wrought in the depths of the earth. Thine eyes have seen my unformed substance" (Psalm 139:13, 15-16).

## WE WERE DESIGNED FOR A PURPOSE

The Lord told Jeremiah, "Behold, like the clay in the potter's hand, so are you in My hand" (Jeremiah 18:6). God had a lesson for Jeremiah, the house of Israel, and for us when he said, "Arise and go down to the potter's house, and there I shall announce My words to you."

Let's take a walk into the potter's house and see what God has to say to us there. We'll need to lower our heads a bit to get through the door. Remember, people were smaller back then. Take a deep breath and smell the wet clay. Look at all the shelves filled with wonderful pots in various stages of completion. What an assortment of pots, jars, bowls, and vessels. Each one is amazingly unique. No mass production line here.

All of the pots are functional, yet all of them are quite beautiful. None of the vessels in Jeremiah's day was *just* a clay pot. Each was a work of art—not like today when we use brown paper bags for lunches, and plastic bags for leftovers, and build museums to display ceramic food as art.

Imagine yourself as a pot. What kind would you be? Perhaps you might think of yourself as one of the large, important vessels that were used as water jars to sustain life, quench the thirsty, and give nourishment to growing things. Or maybe you would be a tall vessel that was filled with wine and brought gladness to the heart. You might be that uniquely shaped vessel that held oil to give light in a dark world. Or, perhaps you might be one of the strong and sturdy vessels that held grain, flour, and oil to feed the hungry. There were also the small bottles to hold exotic fragrances, to fill the air with perfume and draw people closer to them. Perhaps you would be a very special vessel, the one designed to contain a most important item—salt, which was used to season, to preserve, and to heal. And, of course there were the very tiny vials called tear bottles, which were meant to hold the tears and bear the pain of others. What kind of vessel has God designed you to be?

We see the Master Potter working at the wheel. He takes a shapeless lump of clay and envisions what He desires for us to become. He sees our potential, our usefulness, our individuality, and we take on form as He lovingly molds us in His hands and places eternity in our heart. Then God names us. He gives us His identity. "This one will be 'the salt of the earth.' This one over here 'the light of the world.' Ah, and that one, 'the fragrance of Christ.'"

If the clay is too dry and hard, it will break apart, have cracks and slow leaks so that it can't be used for the designed purpose. We must be as moist clay in the Master Potter's hand—yielded, malleable, and surrendered to His will. The quality of the clay of our life determines what the Potter can do with us. What is the quality of your earthen vessel? Take a moment and ask God to show you what keeps you from fulfilling His plan for your life. Remember the defects are in the clay, not in the hands of the Potter.

What about all that debris in our life that keeps us from being all the vessel God planned for us to be? Those impurities sometimes resist the shaping hand of the Master Potter, so the clay has to be cleansed. He's noticed that we have a few odd-shaped pieces of jealousy, a chunk of rebellion, and some rather large hunks of selfishness and greed. They have to go. God is in the business of cleansing impurities from lumps of clay. He says, "'Come now, and let us reason together,' says the LORD, 'though your sins are as scarlet, they will be as white as snow; though they are red like crimson, they will be like wool'" (Isaiah 1:18). He has promised that "If we confess our sins, He is faithful and righteous to forgive us our sins and to cleanse us from all unrighteousness" (1 John 1:9).

## TREASURE IN EARTHEN VESSELS

The apostle Paul also compared us to jars of clay: "We have this treasure in earthen vessels, that the surpassing greatness of the power may be of God and not from ourselves" (2 Corinthians 4:7). When Paul wrote this, he knew that the real treasure was Christ and that he was just an earthen vessel bearing Christ. Believers have this treasure, which is Christ, in our earthen vessels. Our vessels are not made of gold, yet hold wealth untold. Is this a description of your life? In many countries of the world, there is still a custom to hide valuable items such as jewelry or money in clay pots. After all, who would think of looking for valuable treasures in earthen vessels? We hold the greatest treasure within us, regardless of the shape of our vessel.

This was powerfully illustrated for me recently. We were out to dinner with some friends, and the host, Ken, and his brother Rick brought their aged mother along. She had suffered from a stroke and was paralyzed on her right side. That night we witnessed a tender, touching, and heart-wrenching sight. Their mother could walk with a cane and some help, but the only words she could speak were "All right." And that's what she said all night long. She, of course, understood our conversation and often would throw her head back and laugh heartily. She needed her mouth wiped, her food cut up, and to be taken to the bathroom. All the while this dear woman said repeatedly, "All right." Robert and I were so moved by the manner in which these devoted sons treated their mother. They held her hand, kissed her cheek, and cleaned up her spills. Rick said, "After all my mother has done for me, how could I be any other way?" These hard-driving, strong-willed, aggressive men were kind, tender, gentle, patient, loving, and long-suffering with their mother because within that earthen vessel was a great treasure.

There are some in the world who don't celebrate life as God does, and they say, "Get rid of it. It's frayed around the edges, serves no useful purpose, is inconvenient, is no longer attractive, and takes up space." God replies, "You, dear woman, are a woman of worth. Because I have loved you, you are valuable in My eyes. I have a grand purpose for your life. I have created My delightful song in your laugh, My strength in your weakness, and My Spirit in yours."

Some of us have counted our years and announced, "Surely this body and mind are no work of art. They're far too old and move too slow to be regarded by others or used by God." And He speaks from heaven, "It's not how old you are that counts; it's how you are old. I do not measure your worth in years." Scripture tells us in Psalm 139 that even before we were born and began to breathe, He scheduled each day of our life, and He recorded them in His Book.

## WE ARE VALUABLE TO GOD

At the tender age of seven, my daughter Shannon displayed quite an interest and ability in sewing. She decided to surprise me with the gift of an apron that she handmade out of various fabric remnants. After carefully searching and choosing only the most "colorful" and "brilliant" polyester fabrics she could find, Shannon constructed an "apron of many colors." One remnant is shocking pink with teal, navy blue, and chartreuse stripes. Another is an orange, fuchsia, and yellow plaid number. The apron is constructed out of no less than sixteen pieces of these splendiferous colors!

Each piece was cut with great care, though it is not necessarily precise. Each piece was laid in place with the eagerness of a young heart, though it is not necessarily even. Each piece was sewn with childlike delight, though it is not necessarily straight. Shannon pondered over her work until it was exactly the way she envisioned. Such was this labor of love designed to please the object of her affection—me! Did I love it? Yes! Did I wear it? Absolutely! Do I still treasure it after twenty-two years? You bet I do!

Here's the rub. When we were in the process of moving several years ago, one of my helpers suggested that I trash this, this "thing." "Get rid of anything that serves no useful purpose." Unthinkable! This served a purpose so deep, so broad, and so high that I could not measure it. How does one measure a labor of love from a loved one? In cold hard cash? But some in the world say, "When it gets frayed around the edges, serves no useful purpose, is inconvenient, no longer attractive, and takes up space get rid of it." No matter our condition, character, or coherence, God still sees us as valuable, useful, and delightful to Him. That's who God sees.

You are not loved by God because you are valuable, but you are valuable because He loves you. God does not love you because you are so very lovable. Some may sing out, "I'm so wonderful God can't help Himself." But God is very mindful of who we are. We do sin; He just happens to love sinners. God hates the sin but loves the sinner. God takes sinners when they offer their life to Him, and He begins to create something new and beautiful in them. When our lives have been the work of our own hands, look at the mess we have made. But when we have given our life to Jesus, we are the work of God.

Ian Pitt Watson, a charming Scottish theology professor, tells a wonderful story about his daughter,

Rosemarie. At three years old Rosemarie traveled with her parents from England to Australia, which was quite a long plane ride for such a young child. When they arrived in Sydney, a thoughtful member of the welcoming party presented Rosemarie with a rag doll. She was very tired and quietly weeping, so she took the rag doll to bed with her that first night, mopping up the tears. The next night the tears were gone but not the rag doll, nor the next night, nor the next. This doll became the most precious of all Rosemarie's possessions.

As the years went by, it became more and more rag and less and less doll. Actually it was just a bundle of torn up old rags. The logical thing to do was to throw it away. That was unthinkable! You see, if you loved Rosemarie, you loved her rag doll. It was a package deal. What was no better than a bundle of rags was precious in the eyes of Rosemarie.

The world often looks upon people as rag dolls, just trash. The world sees value in lovely things and lovely people. God's love isn't like that; rather He creates value in those He loves—those who receive His love. You bear the identity "God's Work of Art." Allow Him to fashion His work of art in you. You are indeed cherished by your Designer.

## LOVE NOTE TO GOD

Dear Lord, sometimes I don't feel much like a work of art, and sometimes I don't feel valued. And there certainly are times I don't feel I am an earthen vessel that holds a great treasure. But You have said in Your Word that I am all of these things. Forgive me for my arrogance in choosing to believe my own changeable feelings and not Your truth. Teach me to tell myself the truth. Teach me, O God, to see myself as You see me—a person of worth. Teach me also to see the inestimable worth of others.

Love,
Me

## TELLING YOURSELF THE TRUTH

1. Was there ever anything in your life that someone else wanted to "trash" but was valuable to you? How did it become so valuable?

2. List the ways that three different people have demonstrated love for you. Describe what God has done to show how He loves and values you.

3. Have you ever created a good work of art (crafts, painting, sewing, etc.)? What emotions were involved in creating it? How did you feel about the completed piece? What was the reaction of others? Why do we sometimes doubt God's truth about ourselves? If you really believed you were God's "Work of Art," how would that change your self-image and identity?

4. List three reasons why God considers all human life valuable. Why do some not consider all human life valuable?

5. "For by grace you have been saved through faith; and that not of yourselves, it is the gift of God; not as a result of works, that no one should boast" (Ephesians 2:8-9).

"Humble yourselves in the presence of the Lord, and He will exalt you" (James 4:10).

How do we acquire a sense of significance without becoming prideful and arrogant?

6. God said to Jeremiah the prophet: "Before I formed you in the womb I knew you, and before you were born, I consecrated you" (Jeremiah 1:5).

How long has God known you? When did He make plans for your life? What difference does this make to you? How can you apply this verse to your own life?

7. What kind of earthen vessel/clay pot has God designed for you to be? How do you think you are fulfilling God's plan for your life?

8. What impurities or debris are in your "lump of clay" and need "to go"? What are you going to do about it?

9. "If any man is in Christ, he is a new creature; the old things passed away; behold, new things have come" (2 Corinthians 5:17).

If you are "in Christ," how are you personally a "new creation"? What is meant by "old things"? What "new things" are in your life?

10. Describe what happens to the value of human life when people love things and use people instead of using things and loving people. Can you think of any examples?

# 6

## THE FEW, THE FREE, THE FORGIVEN

In the opening scene a turbulent river is flowing through a dense rain forest in South America. Plunging through the violent rapids, a rough-hewn cross bears a martyred Jesuit priest tightly bound to it. He crashes against the rocks and is battered and torn by the churning waters. In one breathless, terror-stricken moment the priest, still fastened to the cross, plunges two hundred feet down a roaring, thundering waterfall. One is immediately held in the grip of this magnetic film, *The Mission*, the story of a man of the sword and a man of the cloth who knit their lives together to protect a South American Indian tribe from subjugation by eighteenth century colonial power mongers.

The man of the sword, Rodriguez, played by Robert DeNiro, is an Indian slave trader and mercenary who murders his brother in a jealous rage over a woman. Rodriguez is greatly grieved and repentant, and although he confesses his sin, he still does not believe he is free from God's condemnation. To do penance for his sin he takes an enormous net (the same one he used to catch the Indians) and fills it with heavy rocks, swords, and armor. In a grueling journey up the edge of the waterfall he carries this crushing load over his shoulder. He drags it, pulls it, heaves it, and wrenches it from twisted foliage and gathering debris, but he will not let go.

One of the priests traveling with him says, "He's had enough!" and takes out his knife and cuts the rope from around his neck. But Rodriguez does not think that he has had enough and runs after the load as it slides down the steep, muddy slope. He reties the rope around his neck and continues up the cliff. The man of the sword insists on carrying his bag of guilt and condemnation up the falls.

When they reach the top, the Indians greet them. Then one man of the very Indian tribe he used to capture can bear watching this sweating, exhausted traveler no longer. He begins hacking at the rope with his hunting knife and sets Rodriguez free from that excruciating load. Free, as we watch the burden tumble down the cliffs and crash into the river below. Free from this outward expression of inward anguish. Free to begin a new life with the guilt of his sin removed.

Jesus did the same thing for us; we need not carry our load of guilt through life. Christ, sweating drops of blood, cut the burden from our backs, not with a knife but with iron spikes on a rough-hewn cross. We, as forgiven, repentant sinners, are "free." With this freedom God gives us an opportunity to be one of His successes.

## BAGGAGE OF OUR OWN CHOOSING

Some of us have a lot of self-condemnation and guilt that we're dragging along life's path. Perhaps we have been involved in adultery, abortion, drunkenness, fornication, gluttony, drug abuse, lying, cheating, stealing, gossip, ungodly behavior, or maybe even murder. Whatever our past sins were, if we have sought forgiveness from the Lord, we are "forgiven." This is our identity; this is who He calls us—"free and forgiven." Jesus Christ has freed us from sin. We can let it all go and be free as He has called us to be. Free to fulfill God's plan for our life. This is who God sees!

If it is our sincere desire to know and celebrate our true identity, then we must face the fact that we often thwart our God-given potential to fulfill our identity. We load ourselves down with bricks of guilt, pride, fear, anger, hate, bitterness, lack of forgiveness, negative thinking, distorted identities, false labels, and resentment. The result, among other things, is low self-esteem. How can we be all that God meant us to be when we're still carrying such excruciating burdens?

Dr. James Dobson describes a person with low self-esteem as a weary traveler on the road of life, dragging along all the garbage of his past. Over his shoulder is a mile-long chain to which is attached tons of scrap iron, old tires, and all kinds of garbage. Each piece of junk is inscribed with the details of some humiliation, a failure, an embarrassment, a rejection from the past. He could let go of the chain and free himself from that heavy load that immobilizes and exhausts him, but he is somehow convinced that it must be dragged throughout life. He is paralyzed by its weight. So he plods onward, digging a furrow in the good earth as he goes.[1] Does this describe you? What kind of baggage are you dragging along through life? The time has come to have that baggage hacked off your shoulders. Jesus says. "Come to Me, all who are weary and heavy-laden, and I will give you rest.

Take My yoke upon you, and learn from Me, for I am gentle and humble in heart; and you shall find rest for your souls. For My yoke is easy, and My load is light" (Matthew 11:28-30).

## OUR DRUG OF CHOICE

Ironically, it's in our very search for freedom that we often place baggage on our back. Perhaps it began when we were teenagers. Our friends smuggled a pack of cigarettes out of the house, and we decided to take our first drag. Freedom at last to act like a grownup. We didn't really enjoy it, but we wanted to be cool. So cool, in fact, that eventually one cigarette a day wasn't quite enough. Then one pack a day wasn't either. Those cigarettes had become a master over us.

Or perhaps it began when our good friends said, "Hey, just one joint won't hurt,"—or one line, one pill, one more drink. "It's the greatest freedom in the world! We'll feel invincible, powerful, and in control." But as we face our third DUI and admittance into the rehab center, we begin to acknowledge that our life has become unmanageable.

We were going to be free, in control, powerful, indomitable, but we surrendered to our drug of choice, whether it was alcohol, drugs, food, sex, clothes, sports, money, career, material possessions, or other people's approval. What "drug of choice" is master over you? Identify it. Give it a name. Perhaps you need to acknowledge that your life has become unmanageable and call upon the Holy Spirit's power to change you from the inside out. He's in the business of redeeming lives. That's the beginning of your becoming master over your appetites and experiencing the freedom that God promises.

I am not a stranger to drug and alcohol abuse. I have witnessed the empty faces and broken lives in families, support groups, and rehabilitation centers. Some of those people have been part of my life and I have loved them. I understand and have experienced the pain as well as the hope of those lives. And on the way to recovery, their desperate heart-cry seemed to be feelings of unworthiness and inferiority. In His Word God gives assurance over and over again of His opinion of us. He holds freedom out to all who would take it, an abundant life to all who surrender to Him, and an identity of inestimable worth to all who believe.

## SURRENDER IS A DOOR TO FREEDOM

The point of surrender can be the door to freedom. The young woman in this story sought freedom, yet her identity was locked up in slavery—slavery to alcohol. She was a wife, a mother, and a homemaker, but her life was a nightmare. She first began drinking alcohol in her home, alone, as a means of temporary release, as a means of getting a little extra sleep. Innocent enough. She had problems. A little brandy or a little wine now and then could certainly hurt no one. She *had* to sleep, she *had* to relax, she *had* to clear her mind and free herself from worry.

But eventually she couldn't live without it. She cared nothing for her personal appearance and took baths only because she could be alone with her bottle. How she ran her home she really didn't know. She realized what she was becoming, and she hated herself for it. She was bitter and angry and blamed everyone and everything but the fact that she could not stop drinking. She discovered that an alcoholic cannot "fight" alcohol.

She threw herself into community activities, volunteering for every organization that would have her. As long as she was busy, she didn't drink, but she always craved that next drink. For an alcoholic, mere cessation is not enough while the need for a drink continues. She couldn't live with alcohol and then discovered she couldn't live without it. She joined A.A. and for the first time in her life reached the point of surrender: "Surrender to me has meant the ability to run my home, to face my responsibilities as they should be faced, to take life as it comes to me day by day, and work my problems out....I had never (before) found or known faith in the reality of God, the reality of His power that is now with me in everything I do" (italics mine).[2]

How interesting that surrender is the way to freedom. This woman discovered her real identity through the act of surrender. Leo Tolstoy said, "We can change the time on a clock either by moving the hands or by moving the main wheel. It is better to change the time by moving the inner mechanism." So also the lives of people.

How will we have a healthy sense of self-worth if we are a slave to anything? Sin can have power over us, but Jesus can set us free from the power of sin. He said, "If therefore the Son [Jesus] shall make you free, you shall be free indeed" (John 8:36). We must believe the truth about what God says. Only we can make that choice. We can choose to stay in the bondage of lies or embrace the freedom that His truth brings.

## A SLAVE TO OTHER PEOPLE'S OPINIONS

Perhaps the cruelest of misused, mistaken, and misrepresented identity is that of being a slave to other people's opinions. It begins early in life and often becomes a way of life. Lydia moved to a new city with her mother and father. She tried very hard to be liked and accepted at the new junior high. Because she was so pretty, she was quickly noticed by the eighth grade boys. The majority of girls rejected her since not only was she pretty but she was also "one of the guys." Playing basketball and running track were second nature to her. When cheerleading tryouts came up, Lydia was so excited. She was well coordinated, knew the cheers, and had a great smile and lots of enthusiasm. If she could just make the team, then surely the girls would accept her. But the eighth grade girls voted on the new cheerleaders, and Lydia didn't make the cut. Lydia stopped playing basketball and gossiped with the girls instead.

In high school she met the man of her dreams and fell head over heels "in like" with him. But a sweet, young, blonde thing caught his eye, and the romance was over. If only she were a blonde! Lydia cried her heart out. Her parents were most supportive, but it wasn't enough for a young girl of sixteen. Lydia became a blonde.

Upon entering college Lydia went through sorority rush. Her first choice was not theirs. She didn't wear the right designer labels. She began to shop for labels.

Lydia volunteered to work for a Christian ministry. She closely watched the other young women, who all seemed to dress like little Laura Ashley models. She saw the mold and poured herself into it. Lydia failed to see herself as unique and acceptable to God. She tried to please God's people, but didn't allow for their humanness. It was there she met a man who encouraged her to study the Scriptures. How she admired his zeal for the Lord! She was diligent in her studies. She wanted him to see her commitment.

When he stepped over the line in their relationship, Lydia was crushed, disillusioned, and devastated. The Laura Ashley crowd shunned her. She decided it was too difficult to please God and His people. She walked away from both and chose to seek the world's approval again.

Lydia was an extremely beautiful girl. All heads turned when she walked by, but in her heart she still didn't measure up. She then met a young man who claimed he loved her, but he didn't always like the way she wore her hair, the messiness of her apartment, her friendly attitude toward others, the sweats she sometimes ran around in, or her choice of dresses. If only he could make her see that his way would be best for her. And oh how he admired ultraslim women! Lydia, who was a size six, became a size four. She changed her hair, organized her apartment, adjusted her attitude, stopped wearing her sweats, and always asked for his opinion first. Why, she wondered, was she so unhappy?

Lydia's greatest mistake was forsaking God. She didn't understand that she could never please the world. It would always demand more and more from her. But God would never leave her side. He was and is the only one who would fully accept her just as she was. It was God alone who would love her unconditionally. It is God who today still seeks after His dear little lost lamb.

Lydia's identity was at the mercy of so many other people's opinions that she became fragmented and had long since lost her true identity. At age thirty life for Lydia had become just a series of people-pleasing decisions that inevitably led to disappointment. It was cruel slavery, but self-inflicted. How many of us can relate and are caught up in this very same trap? The thing that really matters in life is what God thinks, not what we or others think. We need to redefine ourselves from God's perspective. We need to tell ourselves the truth. What is truth? It is Christ in us. It is the people God sees. Nothing more, nothing less. But we must be ready to let go of those chains that have kept us from being "free." The choice is ours.

## "ME NO CRAZY. THIS NUTHOUSE."

*Time* magazine printed an article about a Chinese immigrant named David Tom. Tom suffered from tuberculosis and was admitted to a TB sanitarium. He spoke in the Cantonese dialect, and since no one could understand what he was saying, they diagnosed him as a retarded schizophrenic. He was admitted to an Illinois mental institute in 1952. He knew only a few English words, and he used them, "Me no crazy. This nuthouse."

Nearly thirty years went by, and still no one who could speak his dialect ever examined him. A social worker interested in David took him to a Chinese restaurant where he had the opportunity to speak to the cook in Cantonese. The cook must have been totally shocked when he heard David's story; certainly this man was not retarded. The cook then spoke to the hospital staff, and after an arduous four-year battle in the courts, David was released. Finally, David Tom at age fifty-four was given his freedom from the Illinois State Psychiatric Institute in Chicago. We shrink in horror to think that this kind of bondage can take place today. Yet David Tom was not so unusual in that he was held prisoner by other people's opinions. It was the truth that eventually set him free!

## TIME FOR A RADICAL DECISION

Perhaps the time has come for a radical decision in your life. If the tumor in your lungs is as big as a baseball, limiting your smoking to one pack of cigarettes a day won't cut it. If the floodwaters have risen above your window sills, your home needs more than a light dusting. If your boat has a gaping hole, is taking on water, and the storm is becoming more violent, it's time to do more than comment on the weather. And if you've been carrying a heavy load of guilt and failure, it's time to leave it behind.

Right now, think of some baggage that you need to get rid of. Take just a moment and talk to the Lord. Give it to Him; our shoulders were not designed to carry this weighty load. "Lord, I've been carrying this long enough; it is too heavy and too burdensome for me. I give it to you." Then leave it there. Don't do a "DeNiro," running back to retrieve your burden and retying the rope around your neck. Christ's desire is for us to experience the identities "free" and "forgiven."

## FEW CHOOSE THE PATH

The title of this chapter, "The Few, the Free, the Forgiven," sounds rather like an advertisement for the Marines—"The few, the proud, the Marines." Maybe that slogan isn't too far off from our subject matter here. The Marines don't take just anyone. Applicants must pass some very stringent requirements. Out of many who apply only a few are selected. "The few" also applies to believers. Christians are among "the few," but the difference is that few choose the path, although many are called. Jesus said, "Enter by the narrow gate; for the gate is wide, and the way is broad that leads to destruction, and *many* are those who enter by it. For the gate is small, and the way is narrow that leads to life, and *few* are those who find it" (Matthew 7:13-14, italics mine).

Do you bear the identity "few"? Maybe one day you walked down an aisle at a Billy Graham Crusade, or in a little country church, or at summer Bible camp. Or perhaps it was in the quiet of your study or lying on your bed at night when you realized that you had come to the end of yourself and said yes to Jesus and no to the world. You made a decision to commit your life to Jesus, and then you discovered it wasn't a popular one. But God applauds, congratulates, and cheers you on, for you are numbered among the "few" who choose the small gate and the narrow way that lead to freedom and forgiveness.

## FREEDOM IN KNEE-SOCKS

Have you ever been to a discount-store dressing room? We have a Loehmann's near our home, and I frequently seek its company when I need a support group and some in-depth therapy. There is something wonderful about a roomful of women in their slips and knee-socks, looking for the ultimate buy of the year. We are in this together. No longer can we hide behind the facade of tent tops and long jackets. The illusions that separate us are stripped away. It is so freeing! I have to admit I was embarrassed at first, but I came to realize it was pride and pride alone that kept me from this unique sorority. I have met some of the most endearing women in the vast open dressing room of Loehmann's whom I might never recognize in the grocery store without their knee-socks.

One afternoon in the dressing room a very large woman asked an opinion about a brightly flowered dress with enormous fuchsia cabbage roses on it. "Do you think it's too much?" she questioned. A chorus of replies came, gently encouraging her not to purchase it. One woman quickly left the room and brought back a wonderfully suitable outfit for her. We laughed, we offered advice, and we lamented about feeling "lumpy." We all left with a spring in our step and a new resolve to skip dessert. As I drove away that afternoon with a picture of the dressing room in my mind, I thought, This is the me God sees! No facades, no illusions, and nothing hidden. And you know what, Roberta? He's crazy about you just the way you are. That's freedom!"

## CHAINED TO A PATTERN OF THINKING

Many circus elephants spend their lives chained to a stake in the ground. When they are babies, a large chain is tied to their leg. The little elephant tries with all its strength to get free, but the chain is far too strong for those young legs, and the stake is driven securely into the ground. A pattern of thinking begins to emerge—I'll never get myself free, no matter how hard I try. It's stronger than I am.

As time passes, that little guy loads up on gourmet "elephant food." He now weighs several tons, yet is still chained to the same stake. It would be no problem to give it one swift kick and be off. But he has programmed himself for failure and has given up trying to gain freedom. He made up his mind long ago, "Things will not change. Where I am, I am."

You, child of God, are chained only by the iron rings of your own making. God has called you to be "free" and "forgiven." This is your true identity. These are your names.

## LOVE NOTE TO GOD

Father, forgive me for trying to seek the approval of others. All the while I have been ignoring You. I admit that I have been a slave to _____ in my life. I am powerless over my destructive behavior. Lord Jesus, in You and You alone can I experience victory. I turn my life over to your safekeeping. Your will be done.

Love,
Me

---

## TELLING YOURSELF THE TRUTH

1. In what ways have you experienced the Christian life to be a narrow way? Is it stifling your development as a person? Why or why not?

2. Have you ever been locked out of your house or office? Describe your feelings. What doors of opportunity have been closed to you? What was that like?

3. Have you ever had to acknowledge that your life has become unmanageable? What did you do about it? Was the unmanageable part of your life your master? Have you surrendered it to God? What brought you to that point?

4. Define *surrender* in your own words. How could it be the way to freedom?

5. "Come to Me, all who are weary and heavy-laden, and I will give you rest. Take My yoke upon you, and learn from Me, for I am gentle and humble in

heart; and you shall find rest for your souls. For My yoke is easy, and My load is light" (Matthew 11:28-30).

Why would you exchange your burdens for Jesus' yoke? The Christian walk is not an easy one, so why does Jesus say, "My yoke is easy, and My load is light"? What kind of rest can He give us if we still have to carry a yoke?

6. "If the Son shall make you free, you shall be free indeed" (John 8:36).

How has the Son made you free? What do you think is meant by "free indeed," why not just "free"? If the Son has made you free, why do you still sin? Why are you still a slave to some things? How can you experience the kind of freedom that Jesus offers?

7. "My grace is sufficient for you, for power is perfected in weakness. Most gladly, therefore, I will rather boast about my weaknesses, that the power of Christ may dwell in me" (2 Corinthians 12:9).

What was more important to the apostle Paul than his weaknesses? What can God do with our weaknesses if we surrender them to Him? Are you willing to let Him have them? What is it that will give you success in this?

8. "The LORD redeems the soul of His servants; and none of those who take refuge in Him will be condemned" (Psalm 34:22).

Will God take you back even if you once rejected Him? What kind of person will God condemn?

9. "Trust in the LORD with all your heart, and do not lean on your own understanding. In all your ways

acknowledge Him, and He will make your paths straight" (Proverbs 3:5-6).

How do you use your mind if you trust in the Lord with "all your heart" and "do not lean on your own understanding"? How can you acknowledge God "in all your ways"? What practical difference will this make in your life?

10. In this section, "Telling Yourself the Truth," what have you learned that if applied to your life could give you a sure sense of identity?

# 7

## FAITH WALKING PEOPLE

The trading post opens very early in the morning, just as the sun crests the rugged mountain slopes. Thousands of eager shoppers frantically rush in to be the first to claim their find, their faces intent on the task at hand. I've never seen a market with such peculiar things. Nothing ever goes on sale. Everyone willingly pays full price. Don't look for any bargains or bartering here.

Though you may not realize it, you've been to this trading post. And you've made a fair number of purchases. Paid a handsome price too, I might add. The trading post has a thriving business, but whatever business you conduct, it will cost you dearly. Sometimes it's your dignity and other times your hope. But you always trade the truth for a lie, and faith for fear.

The business for the day looks something like this: You traded your God-given potential for fear of rejection, your true identity for the world's opinions, and your faith for fear.

Been shopping there lately?

## FEAR-STRICKEN PEOPLE

Nike (the athletic shoe company), the "Just Do It!" people, has run some thought-provoking ads. They tell us, "You may not feel like running, jogging, walking, or working out, but 'Just Do It!'" Not bad advice. But, just what is it that keeps us from "just doing it"? What is it that keeps us from meeting certain challenges in life?

Nike ran an ad about fear that went something like this:

Fear of failure. Fear of success.

Fear of losing your health. Fear of losing your mind.

Fear of being taken too seriously.

Fear of not being taken seriously enough.

Fear that you worry too much. Fear that you don't worry enough.

Your mother's fear—you'll never marry.

Your father's fear—that you will marry.

Let me add some others: Fear of rejection. Fear of acceptance. Fear of trying. Fear of not trying. Fear of giving. Fear of receiving. Fear of living. Fear of dying. Fear of loving. Fear of not being loved. Fear of being fearful.

Ever wrestle with any of these? How can we fulfill our God-given potential if we're fearful and afraid of rejection? We're sure that we're not competent enough, creative enough, or capable enough, so we're afraid to try because we know we'll be rejected. Who among us enjoys being rejected?

Public speakers get a lot of rejection. When I stand up before an audience, I know what they're thinking. "I'll give her two minutes. She better give me a reason to listen, or I'm history." I know that's true, because I've thought the very same thing. Have you ever had a deathly fear of making a speech? Perhaps you said, "If I have to get up in front of all those people, I'll die. They'll just scrape me up from the podium and cart my limp body off." Have you ever heard of Arthur MacArthur, the former governor of Kentucky, or Alben Barkley, who was vice president of the United States in 1949? They both died giving a speech. They are the only two people in recent history who gave up their lives at the podium, so the odds are good that you'll live.

## WHAT IF

I came across an acrostic on fear: FEAR—False Evidence Appearing Real. All of our fears are so seldom realized. Yet our fears block our walk of faith. The fears and the "what ifs" in life can do us in.

What if...

> my child is never toilet trained? my husband never grows up?
>
> my car won't start? my car won't stop? I can't find my car?
>
> my boss fires me? my job is phased out?
>
> my spouse leaves me? I get pregnant? I don't get pregnant?

I get cancer? I need surgery? my insurance is canceled?

I lose my hair? it starts growing on my face?

my shoulder pad falls to my chest, the spandex fails in my nylons, parsley sticks to my teeth, and I forget my speech?

We often allow the "what ifs" in life to rob us of our identity as "faith walking people." Some dear friends, John and Terri, lived in a lovely home that they were very content with. One Saturday morning Terri woke up in horror to find their thirty-five-foot eucalyptus tree gone. The homeowners' association had decided to remove all the eucalyptus trees in the common areas of the neighborhood because the enormous roots were causing serious problems, but no one bothered to tell Terri and John. Terri was so distressed that she started to cry, "John, our tree is gone. Our tree is gone!" When John got up to look, all that was left of their wonderful tree was a scrawny, stubby stump. That gorgeous, shady tree was no more.

Then he saw it. A hideous sight he had never noticed before—the sanitation Dumpster. It was now the only thing they saw from the front window of their home. They hadn't noticed it before because the leaves of the eucalyptus kept it from view. Fear quickly overcame John, and his thought process went something like this: "I hate the look of this house now. Aesthetically, it is ruined. This will kill the value of our home. It's lost all curb appeal. What if we never get a buyer? What if it never sells? We're trapped in this barren, treeless house for life. What if we have to sell it for less than our mortgage? We'll probably have to give it away. Financially we'll be ruined! We're going under! I can see it as clearly as that Dumpster; we'll be bankrupt."

Now mind you, John went from tree stump to bankruptcy court in less than twenty minutes. Fear had John selling their home for a loss when it was not even listed for sale. John must have arrived at the trading post early that morning and paid a handsome price for his peace of mind.

One week later a beautiful bottlebrush tree was planted in place of the stump at the expense of the homeowners' association, as had been the plan all along. John and Terri did sell their home months later for much more than their mortgage. The "what ifs" never happened.

False Evidence Appearing Real. John is a lover of the Lord, and his true identity is a "faith walking man." However his faith (for twenty minutes or so) was misplaced. It rested in a eucalyptus tree. How comical it seems to us. Yet how many times have we placed our faith in foolish things? What if we could learn to live without the "what ifs"? Then, we would have the opportunity to live up to our name, "faith walking people." We would face our fears head on.

## THE TRUTH THREE TIMES A DAY

My personal life verse is: "I can do all things through Him who strengthens me" (Philippians 4:13). I'd like you to take a moment right now and repeat it three times to yourself. Now believe it; this is God's Word to you and your fears. If you will repeat this verse three times in succession, three times a day, you will be telling yourself the truth at least nine times each day. I'm not a betting woman, but I bet you don't tell yourself the truth that often. This is one of the tools I have used as a "faith walking woman."

## AFRAID TO FAIL

I've discovered that God never calls anyone to a challenging task without first equipping them. About five years ago, I could not type. It's not that I had never tried. Robert figured that I had taken about five different typing courses since high school. I always hated it. I think I had a "mental block" against typing. Actually, I was afraid I couldn't learn. Sounds crazy, but it's true. As soon as my instructor moved off home row, I moved out the door. But five years ago I signed up for a keyboarding course. (That's English for "typing on a computer.") Not only was I going to learn how to type, but I was going to learn about computers as well. Naturally, I hesitated to surprise my husband with the wonderful news of yet another typing class, but somehow I knew this time would be different. I felt compelled to do this thing; I knew I had to type. Oh yes, the added incentive—Robert eventually promised me a computer if I learned.

I convinced my dear friend Kathy to take the class with me. I became obsessed with learning to type. She kept saying, "Roberta, it's only a typing class; let's not get hyper over this." But I was afraid I'd fail again. We encouraged each other, prayed for each other, and we progressed. I'm not going to say it was easy, because it wasn't. We would whimper and whine all the way to the windy prairie of our community college. Here were two adult women saying things like, "Good grief, today we're going to do numbers and symbols. Tomorrow, Q and Z. We're too old for this. They're asking too much of us." My brain strongly resisted this new discipline, saying things like, "You had your chance five times before, Honey, and we were both a lot younger then."

Why did I have to learn to type? And on a computer no less! Einstein got by with paper and pencil. Shakespeare wrote with a goose quill. However, Ivan Boesky and Gordon Gecko used computers, and we know what happened to them. But God knew what He was doing (He has that way about Him) when He placed that overwhelming desire in me. God is so very practical; he wanted me to realize my potential. Typing would help me, but just because God calls us to a task doesn't necessarily mean it's going to be a walk in the park. Today, this book that you hold in your hands is the direct result of God's work in a person who believes that "I can do all things through Christ who strengthens me." It all started when I decided to face my fear and trust God. You know, of course, the only way to overcome your fear is to face it. So "just do it!"

Believers are called a "faith walking people," not a "fear stricken flock." We live by faith, not by sight, and certainly not by fear. "For we walk by faith, not by sight" (2 Corinthians 5:7). The verse doesn't say, "It's a good idea. Here's a great suggestion. Give this a try sometime." It says, "We walk," period. This is what we do. This is who we are. We live with a trust, dependence, confidence, conviction, reliance, and hope in God. If that's who God sees, what keeps me from seeing with His eyes? The truest thing about me is what God sees.

If bumblebees could read, they would be scared to death to leave the hive. Did you know that it has been scientifically proven to be impossible for bumblebees to fly? Aerodynamically they are constructed all wrong. Their bodies are too heavy, and their wings are too light. Never make it off the ground. But no one told the bumblebee. And it just flies. How we need to listen to God, the One who created us and designed the bumblebee. "Walk by faith, not by sight."

## FACE FEAR HEAD ON

I remember the time that I did my first taping session for my Bible study at the cable TV studio. I prayed, "Dear Lord, I didn't ask for this; I wasn't looking for this. Who are these people and what am I doing here?" I was scared to death. Forget the two that died giving a speech at the podium. The crew was about to witness "death by video taping!" As Robert Orben once said, "I haven't been so scared since I donated my body to a medical school and they said they wanted it now!" In the control room they held up five fingers: "Five, four, three, two, one (cardiac arrest). You're on." To say that I prayed my heart out would be grossly understating the situation. But God gave me the courage to face my fear right after I heard, "You're on." Just in the nick of time. Sometimes when we can't run and we can't hide, God whispers, "You, my child, are a faith walking woman. I will enable you. Trust Me."

My fear of failure was an obstacle that I put in my way. I created the obstacle; God didn't. But I recited Philippians 4:13 so often that it became part of me. May I strongly urge you to memorize it. Until it penetrates your inner being. Until its truth plumbs the depths of your heart. Until it fills every fiber of your being. Learn to treasure God's Word in your heart. It's life-changing. It's transforming. It's telling yourself the truth. Isn't it time you started?

I have a younger sister, Pam, whom I am crazy about. Pam is a beautiful seamstress and dress designer. She started a small business designing and sewing leotards for her daughters' gymnastic team. But what she really wanted to do was to sew and design evening wear for the rich and famous. Or at least for those who could pay and aspire to be famous.

When I called her the other day, she told me a new client was coming over. "Tell me about her," I said. "Well, Roberta, I really don't want to take this client. She told me that she will spare no expense to be the 'Belle of the Ball' and wanted me to make it happen. She has a very successful business and is quite prominent in the community." Ah, she can pay, I thought. Pam continued, "But, I'm afraid to do it and I don't think I will. She is going to want something that I can't deliver. She is very fussy." I asked, "How well do you know her?" Pam replied, "Well, I've never met her, but I'm sure I won't be able to please her. You see, she had this nine-foot-tall armoire that was an entertainment center and housed their TV and stereo equipment. They decided to convert it back to an armoire. You know why? So she could use it as her jewelry box! I'm not ready for this!" I couldn't help but laugh. "Pam, let me tell you about the chapter I'm working on. It's about faith. I refuse to believe that my beloved sister is not a "faith walking woman." Pam called later that day to say she had met with her "armoire client" and is taking the job. She is facing her fear with faith. God has gifted her, equipped her, and enabled her, and she decided to tell herself the truth. "I can do all things through Christ, who strengthens me."

111

## LOOK WHO'S TALKING

A "faith walking person" sees the invisible, believes the incredible, and receives the impossible. Is fear the obstacle standing in the way of discovering your full God-given potential and identity? You do not have to put up with fear. Put it away. Fear is an evil enemy. Fear is not of God. As the Scripture says, "For God has not given us a spirit of timidity, but of power and love and discipline (sound mind)" (2 Timothy 1:7).

What is the antidote to fear? Power, love, and discipline. To be effective we need the power of the Holy Spirit, expressed in love. And the deciding element of success or failure is discipline. Since discipline is also translated "sound mind," doesn't it stand to reason that we must think soundly, think the truth? We must think right to act right.

If fear is not given by God, then who does give it? Who makes us fearful by telling us that we are worthless, inadequate, and incompetent? Jesus called Satan a liar in John 8:44, and not just a liar, but the "father of lies." If we're trying to tell ourselves the truth, we better understand who is telling us the lies we've chosen to believe. They are not from God; they are from the Evil One. What can we do about it? We can "submit therefore to God. Resist the devil and he will flee from you" (James 4:7).

This is a two-fold process. First, submitting to God is to yield, to obey, to surrender, to cease resistance, and to abandon ourselves. Is this a description of our lives? Or have we hit upon some missing ingredients? Second, resisting the devil is to stand against, to be in opposition, to refuse to cooperate, and to keep from yielding to. Is this how we handle the lies that he feeds us? When we choose to believe the lies of the Evil One, whom are we having a conversation with? "I'm so inadequate I'll never amount to anything. Let's face it, I'm stupid. I have no real potential. I just take up space on this earth. No one really loves me or ever will love me. I have no reason to go on living." And you say, "Hey that's right." That is conversation from the pit of hell! Watch whom you're talking with. The "father of lies" is alive and well and living in your hometown. Submit to God, resist the devil, tell yourself the truth, and watch your fears fall away.

## NEGATIVE THINKING

It's amazing how negative thinking can change circumstances. During the depression, there was an old man who ran a lunch counter. He was rather fortunate in that he was a little blind and deaf and didn't hear or read about how bad things were. Not knowing about the depression was a good thing for him. He didn't know that his business was supposed to be failing. He kept his stand freshly painted and advertised with pictures of mouth-watering sandwiches. His business was so successful that he was able to send his son to college.

The young son returned at Christmas with that vast wealth of knowledge that always seems to be acquired in the first semester. He decided to share it. "Pop, something's wrong around here. You act as if you didn't know there is a depression." His son told him all about the economy and how businesses were failing everywhere. His father started some negative thinking. "Maybe I won't paint my stand this year. I won't have enough money. I think I better save with the depression going on. I'll cut back on the amount of meat I put in the sandwiches. I can't waste my money

113

advertising, so I think I'll stop. After all no one has any money." Business soon started to fall off. At Easter vacation his son came home again, and the father thanked his son, "What you said about the depression was absolutely true. I can see it in my business. Son, a college education is a great thing!"[1]

Negative thinking and fear did its deadly work on this old man. Are you sometimes paralyzed by these? Are you wasting precious time with negative thinking? Are you procrastinating because of fear? God never intended for you to live that way. Fear a wasted life more than death! Let me repeat that. Fear a wasted life more than death!

That challenge you're facing, that project you haven't started, that class you were going to take, that diet you're still thinking about, those good intentions that have fallen to the wayside—just do it! Face your fears. You may think of yourself as a total failure. That's not in God's vocabulary! We must think no less of ourselves than God thinks. How arrogant of us to deny the identity Almighty God gives us. We are never failures in God's eyes. Friends, I have learned in my own experience that failure is an event in my life; it is not me.

"Failure should be our teacher, not our undertaker. Failure is delay, not defeat. It is a temporary detour, not a dead-end street" (William Ward).

"It is a mistake to believe that a man succeeds through success. More often than not, a man succeeds through failure" (Abraham Lincoln).

## BE A QUITTER!

When we think of ourselves as failures, we may resort to degrading ourselves with negative self-talk. Have you ever called yourself nasty names and really meant it—names like "stupid," "idiot," "dumb," "ugly," "brainless," "loser," or "hopeless case"? Is this God's opinion of us also? Did God tell us to hurl insults at ourselves? He freed us from the sin and guilt of our past, and now we are engaging in self-hate. How can this be? Don't we remember whose we are and who it was that made us? We are a Designer's original, an "Image Bearer of Christ," "Free," "Forgiven," and "Faith Walking Women"! This is the you and me God sees. How differently we would live if we thought of ourselves as God thinks of us.

Today, this moment, make a commitment to yourself and to God. Be a quitter. Quit calling yourself degrading names. Just stop it. If we continually repeat to ourselves negative thoughts, it isn't long before it becomes a self-fulfilling prophecy. "As a man thinks in his heart, so he is." Remember the tattoo, "Born to lose"? Before tattoo on body, tattoo on mind.

But we say, "You don't know me. I'm hopeless. You don't know what I've done, and what I continue to do." When was the last time we heard God say, "Well this is a hopeless case; I give up on this one"? He never gives up. We're never hopeless in His eyes. Faith is remembering we are God's priceless treasure when we feel utterly worthless. But remembering it will make no difference unless we decide to believe it and act on it. The ball is in our court! We must be quitters.

## CHRIST THINKER

Jesus Christ never had a defeated, negative attitude. Jesus was the ultimate in "Faith Walking People." Did you ever read anywhere in the Bible where Jesus whimpers, "I can't do it, it's just too hard, I don't have the resources, I don't have the power, and besides this is an impossible situation. Raise Lazarus, are you kidding! Do you know how many days he's been dead. Feed five thousand people with this little kid's sack lunch? Instead He said and demonstrated that "the things impossible with men are possible with God" (Luke 18:27). It isn't wishful thinking or even positive thinking. It is biblical thinking. It is Christ-like thinking, what I call a "Christ Thinker." It is having the mind of Christ. As 1 Corinthians 2:16 says, "For who has known the mind of the Lord, that he should instruct Him? But we have the mind of Christ."

Did you know, child of God, that your identity is one of being a "Christ Thinker"? Our thoughts are to be according to Jesus Christ, not according to the world. Among other things, a "Christ Thinker" is one who believes that, according to the will of God, "all things are possible to him who believes" (Mark 9:23).

You know, it's not the circumstances facing us today. It is how we deal with them. The negative person views the problem with a hopeless attitude, the "Christ Thinker" with hope. Whether it is a diet, a crumbling marriage, a teenager on drugs, an addiction, a lack of a college degree, sick and aging parents, poor health, an impossible financial condition, sagging self-esteem, or feelings of defeat, worthlessness, hopelessness—all things are under the control of a God who can do impossible things. The world says, "Believe in yourself." Jesus says, "Believe in Me."

I am only as strong as that in which I believe. If I believe only in myself, I am weak and will often fail. But if I believe in Jesus Christ, I will be as strong as He. And He is never weak. He will never fail. In Him all things are possible. The world says, "Show me and I'll believe." Christ says, "Believe Me and I'll show you."

Maybe you're saying, "I can't change. I was raised in a family with photographic minds—always negative. Now it's become a way of life." But don't you know that we're in control of what we think and dwell upon? When a thought comes into our minds, we have the power to remove it. A Chinese proverb says, "That the birds of worry and care fly above your head, this you cannot change. But that they build nests in your hair, this you can prevent." Paul assures us that we can control our thoughts: "We are destroying speculations and every lofty thing raised up against the knowledge of God, and we are taking every thought captive to the obedience of Christ" (2 Corinthians 10:5). When a negative, ungodly thought comes into your mind, choose-to-refuse to consider it. Strive to focus on the Word of God. Replace that thought with Scripture. How about nine times a day of truth telling? Choose not to think of the negatives.

Memorize Scripture. The power of the Word of God hidden in your heart enables you to take every thought captive to the obedience of Jesus Christ, to be a "Faith Walking Woman," to be the person God sees. Our faith is not in our own abilities, but in our great God. Gladys Hunt, a Bible teacher, said it so well: "It is better to have a little faith in a great God than to have great faith in faith."

## TESTED FAITH

What good is a car if it is never driven? How strong are one's legs if they never learned to walk? What good is faith if it isn't tested? Faith is the daring of the soul to go farther than it can see.

The California coast was shrouded in fog that Fourth of July morning in 1952. Florence Chadwick, a thirty-four-year-old woman, waded into the water, determined to be the first woman to swim the twenty-one miles to Catalina Island. She had already been the first woman to swim the English Channel in both directions.

The water was bitter cold, and the fog was so thick she could hardly see the boats in her own party. Millions of people were watching her journey on national television. Sharks came dangerously near and had to be driven away with rifles. Florence swam on tirelessly as the miles were put behind her. Fatigue was rarely a big problem in these swims. It was the bone-chilling cold of the water.

After more than fifteen hours in the water, Florence, numbed by the cold, asked to be taken out. She couldn't go on. Her mother and trainer were alongside her in a boat and called out words of encouragement, "Don't quit now. You're near land. Just hang on. You're almost there." But all she could see was the dense fog.

A few minutes later, at fifteen hours and fifty-five minutes, she was taken out of the water. After her body began to warm up, the shock of failure hit her. As the news reporters questioned her, she blurted out, "Look, I'm not excusing myself. But if I could have seen land, I might have made it."

Florence then realized she had been pulled out only a half-mile from the coast. She admitted she had been licked not by fatigue or even by the cold. It was the fog alone that had defeated her. It had obscured her goal. It had blinded her reason, her eyes, her heart. "I, Florence Chadwick, had quit." Two months later she swam that same channel. The fog again obscured her view, but in her mind's eye she fixed her eyes on the goal. This time she swam with faith. Somewhere beyond that dense fog was land. Florence Chadwick was the first woman to swim the Catalina Channel. Not only that, but she beat the men's record by some two hours.

Let us run with perseverance the race marked out for us, fixing our eyes on Jesus, the author and finisher of our faith. Whether we run this race or walk it, this is not just a single deed or an isolated act. It is a total attitude. It is a way of life—"faith living," "faith acting," "faith thinking," "faith walking."

## NOAH IS ON MY SHORT LIST

Faith calls for and even demands risk. Does the word "risk" make your knees buckle? We will never become strong in our faith if we're not willing to risk, to step out in faith. "Faith walking people" risk their reputations, risk being ridiculed, ignore common sense, and some risk their lives. Oh if we could only be like them! We can be like them. They are common, ordinary people with an extraordinary, uncommon faith. They know God can be trusted.

What kind of risk did Noah experience? Let's face the facts. Common sense did not dictate Noah's decision. They lived five hundred miles from the nearest body of water. It had not rained on the earth up to that time. The Bible says he was building the ark to save his family, but it was gigantic compared to the size of his family. How thrilled do you imagine the neighbors were when eighteen thousand tons of gopher wood were delivered to Noah's driveway? "What a guy. What a man of faith." Hardly. They complained to the homeowners' association. Why then would he build the ark? Would you? Noah built the ark because he believed God. Noah was no weak-willed, wimpy milquetoast! He was brave, bold spirited, and became the best boat-builder in town!

Who said Christianity was for weak people? This life of faith is not for the faint hearted but for the stout hearted. It is not for the cowardly but for the brave. It is not for the fearful but for those few who choose to abandon themselves to the providence of God. "Faith walking people" are not wimps. When men and women of faith come to mind, Noah is on my short list. God gave Noah one hundred and twenty years to build the ark. His walk of faith lasted longer than our lifetime! If faith were the topic of conversation, would your name be brought up?

## WE'RE A STRANGE LOT

I love what A.W. Tozer wrote about faith. "We are a strange lot. A real Christian is an odd number. He feels supreme love for One he has never seen. Talks with familiarity everyday with someone he cannot see. Expects to go to heaven on the virtue of another. Empties himself in order to be filled. Admits he is wrong so he can be declared right. Goes down in order to get up. Is strongest when he is weakest. Richest when he is poorest. Happiest when he feels the worst. He dies so he can live. Forsakes in order to have. Gives away so he can keep. Sees the invisible, hears the inaudible, and knows that which passes understanding!" What better description could there be of "faith walking people"?

## LOVE NOTE TO GOD

Oh Father, I had no idea that I was not trusting you when I gave in to my fears. I never quite thought of myself as a "faith walking person," but that's who You say I am. Please help me to face my fears, to abandon myself into Your safekeeping, to resist the Evil One, and to live as a "Christ Thinker." It sounds like so much, but I know that it boils down to this: Teach me how to walk by faith, not by sight, and to see the me You see. I love You, Lord, for who You are and for what You are doing in my life.

Love,
Me

## TELLING YOURSELF THE TRUTH

1. List three of your most common fears. If fear is "false evidence appearing real," then what is the false evidence about each of your fears?

2. Describe a time in your life when you truly walked by faith and not by sight. How did you feel? Did anyone around you notice that you were different? Did you tell them why? Would you do it again in the same circumstances?

3. Name three things that you are telling yourself the truth about as a result of what you've learned so far. How do you know it's true? Is it Scripture? What difference do you think it will make in your life?

4. Did you ever fail to try something because you had a fear of failure? Was it a real fear or imagined? Did you ever overcome it? What were the results?

5. Name three of your most common "what ifs." Can you prevent any of these from happening? What are you going to do about them?

6. "All things are possible to him who believes" (Mark 9:23).

Think of some synonyms for the word *believe*. What do you think is meant by "to him who believes"? Believes in what? Believes in whom?

7. "For who has known the mind of the Lord, that he should instruct Him? But we have the mind of Christ" (1 Corinthians 2:16).

What is the "mind of Christ"? How do we have it? How can we know that we are thinking like Christ? Why do we not always use the "mind of Christ" in our daily lives?

8. "Now faith is the assurance of things hoped for, the conviction of things not seen" (Hebrews 11:1).

Is faith an imaginary product of your mind? What is it that makes faith real? Has your faith ever been tested? How? Did that prove the validity of your faith?

9. Is the Christian faith a blind faith or is it based on truth? If so, what truth? How would you answer someone who told you that you are living by "blind faith"?

10. Read Hebrews chapter 11, the "faith" chapter. How did these great men and women of the Bible

please God? What or who was the object of their faith? What things or people have you placed your faith in? Have they ever failed you? Has God ever failed those who trusted in Him?

# 8

## The King Is My Father

The other night we rented the movie *The Bear*, an action-packed story about a little grizzly bear cub named Youk and the giant grizzly who befriends him. Orphaned as a little cub, Youk is left to wander the wilderness of British Columbia alone. He is hardly equipped for survival on his own. He is just a baby, still playing with tortoises and butterflies as he investigates his world. He has the most endearing way of speaking in his "little bear noises" of grunts, growls, and gnarls. You can't help but love the little guy.

Early in the story Youk stumbles upon a fierce, roaring, frightening, gigantic male grizzly who has been wounded in the shoulder by a hunter. Youk licks the grizzly's wounds and stays by his side, and the giant becomes his trusted friend. One day as the little cub is scrounging around for a meal on his own, a mountain lion hungrily eyes him. The cat starts after him, and little Youk races with all his heart to escape, but before long the lion corners him on the edge of a cliff. Just as the big cat lunges toward him, the cub finds a tree branch hanging over the cliff. Snarling and hissing, the lion also climbs on the branch and takes a swipe at our frightened friend with his claw-laden paws. The tree branch breaks off, dumping Youk whining and crying into the raging river below. He manages to catch a ride on a log over the swift rapids, but the lion sprints down the riverbank with plans to catch his next meal. Youk's log floats him into shallow water and finally onto dry land where the cat is waiting for him.

You're pulling for the little cub all along. You can't stand the thought of this cat clawing him, but that's precisely what happens. Youk's thinking, I'm history. But I'll give it one big bear try. He stands on his hind legs as he had seen his gigantic friend do, and from the depths of his belly he bellows as fierce a roar as he can muster. "R-O-A-R!" The cat looks incredulous. "Why you little pip squeak!" The cub repeats himself, "R-O-A-R!" Suddenly the lion stops and starts to move backwards.

Youk didn't know he had it in him; now it's war. He throws his little head back and thunders again with all his might, "R-O-A-R!" Youk himself is stunned. That was the grandest growl he'd ever heard. The mountain lion hastily retreats, but it wasn't the fierce roar of Youk that did it. Unbeknownst to the little cub, his gigantic grizzly friend, all eighteen feet of him, is standing on his haunches directly behind him. It was he who growled the frightening roar that sent the lion backtracking. It was he whose shadow stood over the cub and protected him from his enemy. It is a powerful and moving scene.

What a wonderful portrayal of the power and protection of our Heavenly Father. We as "Children of the King" may dwell in our Father's shadow. The psalmist said, "He who dwells in the shelter of the

Most High will abide in the shadow of the Almighty" (Psalm 91:1). There, we may seek safety and protection. God invites us to seek His shelter and experience His provisions.

## NOT AN OVERNIGHT JOB

Remember the day that some of you heard those life-changing words: "I now pronounce you man and wife"? Did you feel completely like a wife? You stood in the reception line and made your first introduction, "I'd like you to meet my husband." It felt perhaps a bit awkward, but great. As a married woman, you received a new name and a new title, a new identity, but it took a while to feel it, to act like it, to really believe it, and to think like a married person. It surely didn't happen overnight. That's how it is when one becomes a child of God. God's work in us is not an overnight job either!

When we first gave our heart to Jesus, most of us probably didn't feel like a full-fledged "Child of the King." This was a new identity, a new title, a new name, and a new life. There was a lot of work to be done. It wasn't going to be an overnight job. But it was truth; it was reality.

A "Child of the King" enjoys and experiences many privileges. To understand our true identity we will explore some of these, such as God's commitment of love to us and how He delights in His children and grieves with us in our sorrows. The Father places resources at His child's disposal and assures us He is a prayer-answering God. But these are not the limits of our privileges and inheritance. There is not enough paper in the world to contain them. Volumes could be written on what our Father has provided for us.

## EARTHLY FATHERS ARE DIFFERENT

Perhaps you have not had a loving, protective earthly father, so the idea of God the Father is not a pleasing one. Your earthly father is not like your Heavenly One. Perhaps your earthly father was never there when you needed him; perhaps he abandoned you or wasn't very understanding, loving, or wise. He may have degraded you, embarrassed you, been unreasonable, or communicated to you that you didn't matter to him. Some of you have hated your own father for being cruel and brutal. Possibly you were abused emotionally, physically, or sexually. Some of you were raised with a father who was an alcoholic or drug addict, and you suffered from his excesses. John Trent, Ph.D., and Gary Smalley, authors of *The Language of Love*, say, "There is a 'father hunger' in many women's hearts today. Instead of recalling tender memories of the first significant man in their life, many look back and see only empty arms and unspoken words of love and acceptance. And in many cases, as the years pass these hurtful memories act like sandpaper on a woman's soul."

No, we all didn't find safety and protection in the presence of our father, and now we're struggling with the concept of God being our Father. "Father" has not been an endearing term to us. But in our God we have the perfect Father who is committed to us. He promises to provide the security, stability, and safety that we may never have experienced. As Romans 8:28 says, "And we know that God causes all things to work together for good to those who love God, to those who are called according to His purpose." This verse doesn't say all things that happened to us are good but that God can and will work things out for the good for those who love Him. That's a wonderful promise!

## A "CHILD OF THE KING" KNOWS THE FATHER'S PROTECTION

God's protection doesn't mean that we are free from disasters, disease, or divorce. It isn't an invisible deflector shield that bounces off all the evils of this world. God will protect us from many of these, but His primary protection is spiritual and eternal.

Sometimes the physical world helps to remind us of things spiritual. I have a wonderful collection of hats in my wardrobe—hats of all sizes and colors for all occasions and weather. I used to wear them occasionally just for fun until my dermatologist discovered a spot diagnosed as basal cell carcinoma (skin cancer). It was quite small and was removed without a problem. My physician warned me, however, to be cautious and protect my skin from the sun. She said, "Roberta, the best protection is a big hat." So I decided to enlarge my inventory. My husband lovingly refers to my hats as the "Mother of all hat collections." In Phoenix we have about 350 days of sunshine a year. (My boundaries have fallen in pleasant places!) So I am very conscientious about wearing one just about everyday.

When I grab a hat and run out the door, I am under the protection of its brim. I have chosen to be under that shade. I am untouched by the sun as long as I choose to keep my hat on. It has become a subtle yet lovely reminder for me that God is my shade, my refuge, and my protector. I have chosen to seek my Father's shelter. God's sheltering hand is a beautiful thing for His children. Just like my hats! Perhaps you have a personal practical reminder of His protection and how He watches over you, His child. How about seat belts, face masks, hard hats, safety shoes, crash helmets, goggles, life preservers, or umbrellas?

Though we are under the watchful eye of the Father's protection, He does allow us to be exposed to attacks from the Evil One that we may grow in Christ-like character. Exposed to attacks? A "Child of the King"? Hey, this isn't the trip I signed up for! The apostle Paul described his life as one full of "dangers from rivers, dangers from robbers, dangers in the city, dangers on the sea, and dangers in the wilderness." Sounds like we'll need those belts, hats, helmets, and life preservers. Where are all the "still waters" and "green pastures"? If we're His children, shouldn't we expect a walk in the park instead of a walk on the wild side? Though our Father is our shield, refuge, and protector, He will not isolate us from the bitter uncertainties of life. However, He guarantees He'll be there to take us through them. After all, He's committed to us.

## A "CHILD OF THE KING" KNOWS THE FATHER'S COMMITMENT OF LOVE

A "Child of the King" knows the Father's love for him. It is like no other love. No human love can compare. His love is not conditional. It doesn't depend on our performance. Many in the world say, "I'll love you if…". If you love me. If you love my friends. If you think like I do. If you speak my language. If you have my skin color. If you go to my church. If you believe as I do. If you do as I do. If you do as I say. I'll love you "if." God's love doesn't demand performance. He loves you because He has chosen to set His heart upon you. No strings attached, no "ifs."

When Robert, my husband, was just a small child, his dad, who played professional baseball, would prop him up against the wall, and they would toss a baseball back and forth. When Robert was old enough, his dad would take him out to the park and spend five to six hours every Saturday and Sunday afternoon practicing. Those were great times for both of them. It was hard work though. Robert didn't always feel like practicing, nor did his father. It didn't matter that Robert couldn't throw, pitch, catch, or bat perfectly each time. His dad's commitment and love didn't depend on performance. But he taught his young son everything he knew and instilled the love of baseball in his heart. He demonstrated commitment to discipline over many weekends and many years.

At sixteen Robert graduated from high school. Several major league teams were after him and offered handsome contracts. How his dad wanted to see him play baseball! Because Robert was under age, his dad would have to sign for him, but he refused, saying, "Son, one of my greatest desires is for you to graduate from college. Then you can play ball if you like." His father was committed to his son's growth and future well-being. He denied him to bring about a greater good. That meant delayed dreams. Robert was very angry at his father for not allowing him to do what he wanted. He was twice the size of his dad, and when he was angry, it wasn't a pretty picture. But obedience had been instilled in him by a father committed to tough love.

When Robert's father passed away nineteen years ago, I remember him saying, "I just wanted to stand up at the funeral service and for all I was worth sing 'Take Me Out to the Ball Game' to my dad one last time! My dad loved me, and he communicated it by his lifelong commitment to me."

When we are young in our faith, our Heavenly Father just gently tosses the ball to us. He patiently waits for teachable moments, because he understands that spiritual maturity takes time. His Holy Spirit instills a love of His Word in our hearts. God doesn't pound his children into submission, but He does discipline us with tough love. And after many Saturdays and many years of practice, we learn obedience and reap its rewards. We pray and beg Him for a contract we're not mature enough to sign. He knows we cannot handle it and sometimes denies us an opportunity, a request, a chance. He watches us struggle through His purposeful plans. We eventually grow to trust His wisdom, and as we mature in Christ, we overflow with love for Him. We find ourselves singing praises for all we're worth to a Father who is wholly committed to us.

## A "CHILD OF THE KING" KNOWS THE FATHER'S DELIGHT

Late one night I was reading by the fireside all alone. I settled in my comfortable, overstuffed chair with the book *The Practice of the Presence of God* by Brother Lawrence. Brother Lawrence was a lay brother among the barefooted Carmelites in the late seventeenth century. He was a simple worker in the kitchen of the monastery; he was not a theologian or a learned scholar. His sole desire in life was to walk in God's presence continually, even amid the pots and pans, preparing meals and washing dishes.

As I was reading this little book, I had been considering the idea of being a child of God and what it meant to me personally. Then I came upon this section where Brother Lawrence speaks about how he considers himself before God, whom he beholds as his King.

> I consider myself as the most wretched of men, full of sores and corruption, and who has committed all sorts of crimes against his King. Touched with a sensible regret, I confess to Him all my wickedness, I ask His forgiveness, I abandon myself in His hands that He may do what He pleases with me. The King, full of mercy and goodness, very far from chastising me, embraces me with love, makes me eat at His table, serves me with His own hands, gives me the key of His treasures; He converses and delights Himself with me incessantly, in a thousand and a thousand ways, and treats me in all respects as His favorite. It is thus I consider myself from time to time in His holy presence.[1]

I set the book aside and said, "That's it! That's it! I knew it. I'm God's favorite!" Now before I go a step further, let me tell you that Scripture states that God shows no partiality and has no favorites. Having said that, let me confess. I've always felt that God my Father treated me as if I were His only child and His favorite. He's always been there when I needed Him. He could be completely trusted. I felt in my heart and knew in my mind that He delighted in me. Aren't you aware when people really love you? Can't you feel their delight and joy? My Heavenly Father treats me as if I were His favorite.

My father did something perhaps a bit unusual with his five children. He took each of us aside and said, "Roberta, you are my favorite child." "Pamela, you are my favorite child." "Joyce, you are my favorite child." "Joan, you are my favorite child." "Bobby, you are my favorite child." None of us knew that he had given the same favor to all his children. What I did know was how special I felt; my father had singled me out for extra attention when he told me I was his favorite. How I treasured this knowledge in my heart! He treated each one of us as if we were his only child and his favorite.

Then one day about five years ago, as Pam and I were talking about our family, she said, "Look, Roberta, you know I always was Dad's favorite." "What?" I was stunned. I said, "I beg your pardon, but I was Dad's favorite!" "Roberta," she assured me, "Dad told me that I was." "But, Pam," I said, "he told me the very same thing. I wonder if you can have more than one favorite?" That's when we began to strongly suspect that each one of us was equally his favorite. How wise of him to treat each of us as if we were his only special child.

That's just what God our Father does! He delights Himself with us incessantly, in a thousand and a thousand ways, and treats us in all respects as His favorite. As Brother Lawrence would say, "It is thus that you must consider yourself from time to time in His holy presence." Tell yourself the truth about how God feels about you.

"The LORD your God is with you, he is mighty to save. He will take great delight in you, he will quiet you with his love, he will rejoice over you with singing" (Zephaniah 3:17, NIV). This verse from Zephaniah describes God much like a loving parent singing a lullaby to a distressed child. Our Heavenly Father is wise, tender, and compassionate. The Lord our God is head over heels in love with us. He is crazy about us! This is truth.

## A "CHILD OF THE KING" HAS ALL THE FATHER'S RESOURCES

A "Child of the King" realizes that the King has all of His resources at His children's disposal. His help, His power, His wisdom, His protection, His everything. There is no room in our lives to say, "I can't do it, I'm afraid, I'm not adequate, I don't have the resources." If God has called us to a task, He will also equip us and enable us. God says, "I know you're not adequate, but I am your adequacy." Jesus Christ is all you'll ever need.

My dear friend Sue was relating a personal story to me after they lost Titus, their three-month-old grandson, to sudden infant death syndrome (SIDS). Their son Steve was a pastor in a small church. Steve, his wife Sydney, Sue, and her husband Bill were taking just a moment to sit down in between making arrangements for the memorial service when there was a knock at the door. A woman was holding a platter of food just in case they needed it. Yes, there was a need. She introduced herself since she was not even a member of the church. But she had heard Steve preach one Sunday and was so touched by his sermon she wanted to do something for the family in their time of need. They never saw her again.

The funeral and ambulance expenses were great for the young pastor. It would put a tremendous strain on their budget at a time when their hearts were breaking with this overwhelming loss. The church secretary called later that day to inform them that an anonymous donor had just given a thousand dollars to pay the funeral expenses. When Steve contacted the ambulance company to pay the balance, they told him there was no record of a balance. It had been paid. Provisions from the heart of the Father. He is generous with His resources.

## A "CHILD OF THE KING" KNOWS THE FATHER ANSWERS PRAYER

We bring to Him our hopes, plans, failures, joys, struggles, and tears. He hears, He listens, He answers, and He never makes a mistake. Our Father is all-wise. Because our Father knows the end from the beginning, He doesn't always answer our prayers as we have requested or when we would like them answered. I had been praying for twelve years for my son Richard Christopher to return to the Lord. I was ready for God to answer my prayer after a week, but God waited over twelve years. There was much heartbreak during those years, but God's timing was perfect. R.C. moved up to Montana, started reading his Bible again, attended a Bible study, and got serious about prayer. How could this possibly happen? I wasn't even there to hang over him and tell him how to do it all. One evening we talked on the phone late into the night as he excitedly related his prayer life to me. For once I was speechless. Here was the evidence that the love of God is between two people—God and the beloved. My role? Praying mother who trusts in a prayer-answering God.

## A "CHILD OF THE KING" KNOWS THE FATHER GRIEVES

Our Father is compassionate and approachable and understands our sorrows. Isaiah 53 says our Lord was "a man of sorrows, and acquainted with grief....Surely our griefs He Himself bore, and our sorrows He carried." Richard Wurmbrand, a prisoner in Communist prisons for fourteen years, experienced a profound way in which God grieved with him. Wurmbrand was a Romanian pastor who was brutally tortured for his faith in and love of Jesus. He tells his heartbreaking story in *Tortured for Christ* and *In God's Underground*. "They broke four vertebrae in my back and many other bones. They carved me in a dozen places. They burned me and cut eighteen holes in my body."[2] Wurmbrand spent three years in solitary confinement. It was there in desperation he cried out to God that he might hear just His voice. Oh that God would speak to Him! It was at that moment he heard the agonized wail of another victim being tortured. Wurmbrand knew in his heart that God had answered his prayer. God felt his anguish, knew his anxiety, identified with his affliction, and wailed in His grief. At that moment he experienced God entering his pain and sharing it with him. It was then his heart rejoiced, for he was not alone. "I will never desert you, nor will I ever forsake you" (Hebrews 13:5c).

## A "CHILD OF THE KING" KNOWS THE PERSON GOD SEES

I was speaking at a retreat on this topic when a sweet, quiet, tender, young woman came up to me afterwards. She introduced herself not with her name or even what she did, but by a series of events in her life. She said, "I'm a battered wife. The last time he beat me it was pretty bad. I'm still black and blue from being punched and kicked. But my husband told me that the Bible said I was to submit to him. So aren't I supposed to?" As I stood there, I could feel the heat of anger rising up my face, but I knew how important it was for me to lovingly communicate help to her at that moment. What I said was "My dear friend, God your Heavenly Father created you to dwell in the shadow of His wings, in safety and under His protection. God never intended for His children to live in a situation of abuse such as you have endured. You must seek help! You, Child of the King, were not meant to live in such terror and dread." She had been abused as a daughter and married a man like her father. She couldn't relate to the concept of a loving Heavenly Father. This young woman's identity in her own eyes was "battered wife" not "Daughter of the King."

We, or someone dear to us, may hold the memory of the terrible tragedy of abuse. But we must not define ourselves as "victims." That is not who we are. It was an event or series of events in one's life. These things keep us from realizing our full identity in Christ. The truest thing about ourselves is what God says. When God lovingly looks upon us, does He see women as doormats? Is the me God sees supposed to submit to battering, beating, and bruising at the hands of another? We are "Children of the King." Nothing can rip that truth from God's heart. Nor should we allow it to be torn from ours. We are His treasured possession, people of worth, of inestimable value, precious in the sight of God.

We must take the steps to be empowered by the God of the universe, instead of being at the mercy of others. There is hope. We matter to God!

We can start by telling ourselves the truth from Scripture. We were once enemies of God; now we are friends. Once we were slaves; now we are adopted children with full rights. Once we were children of darkness; now we are children of light. Once we were foreigners and aliens, now we are members of God's household.

Jesus said, "Unless you turn to God from your sins and become as little children, you will never get into the Kingdom of Heaven. Therefore anyone who humbles himself as this little child, is the greatest in the Kingdom of Heaven" (Matthew 18:2, TLB). Let's consider some common traits of a child. A child is playful, trusting, humble, innocent, forgiving, dependent, vulnerable, spontaneous, loves easily, doesn't worry, is not self-conscious, sleeps peacefully, knows he needs someone bigger than himself, and desires only the basic needs of life. Does that describe you? We're not talking about being childish, but childlike.

Watchman Nee tells of a man who was deeply distressed. "'I am trying to be faithful to God, but I continually fail, no matter how much I pray.' Nee replied, 'Do you see this dog here? He is my dog. He is house-trained; he never makes a mess; he is obedient; he is a pure delight to me. Out in the kitchen I have a son, a baby son. He makes a mess, he throws his food around, he fouls his clothes, he is a total mess. But who is going to inherit my kingdom? Not my dog; my son is my heir. You are Jesus Christ's heir because it is for you that He died.' So it is with us. We are Christ's heirs, not through our perfection but by means of His grace."[3] "The Spirit Himself bears witness with our spirit that we are children of God, and if children, heirs also, heirs of God and fellow heirs with Christ" (Romans 8:16-17).

Once you grab hold of the truth that the most accurate view of you is what God sees, it will change your entire self-image. For you will realize that the only opinion of you that really matters is what God thinks. No longer will the names and identities others have called you destroy your dignity and self-worth. You are a valuable treasure in the eyes of the King, your Father.

## LOVE NOTE TO GOD

Dear Father, there have been times when I have not allowed myself to be loved by You. I was upset, angry, and frustrated, and didn't seek the comfort of Your presence. I was miserable and no one was going to stop me from feeling that way. I didn't know that You were there grieving over my struggles and tragedies with me. I needed to dwell in the shelter of Your protection then, and I need it now. Please give me the sensitivity to feel and to know Your delight in me. I've been disappointed by others in life, and it's difficult for me to really believe that You love me so perfectly, so unconditionally. Teach me to tell myself the truth.

Love,
Me

## TELLING YOURSELF THE TRUTH

1. Describe a time when you were rescued from danger or protected from it. Who rescued or protected you? How did you feel about that person? How did you thank your rescuer? What was his or her reaction?

2. Has the concept of God being your Father been a struggle for you? Why? How was your relationship with your earthly father? What have you never

received from your father that you always longed for? How does that relationship affect your relationship with God?

3. List five benefits and five resources that you have at your disposal as a "Child of the King." Which ones do you act upon most frequently? Which one is the hardest to accept? Why?

4. Have you ever been involved in an abuse situation, as an observer or a victim? Did you take any action? What kind? What were the first signs of abuse toward the victim? What could have been done to avoid further episodes? How would you describe the self-esteem of the victim?

5. Why do we stay in situations that are unhealthy or dangerous? What help, options, or agencies are open to victims of abuse in your community?

6. "He who dwells in the shelter of the Most High will rest in the shadow of the Almighty" (Psalm 91:1, NIV).

Describe what it means to you personally to "dwell in the shelter" and "rest in the shadow." Is "dwell" a word of action and "rest" a word of inaction? Is it possible to dwell and rest at the same time? How?

7. "And we know that God causes all things to work together for good to those who love God, to those who are called according to His purpose" (Romans 8:28).

How many "things" does God cause to work together for good? For whom? Describe a situation in your life when God worked it out for the good. As a result of suffering, how have you or others involved grown spiritually? Are you able to see any purpose to suffering?

8. "Let all bitterness and wrath and anger and clamor and slander be put away from you, along with all malice. And be kind to one another, tender-hearted, forgiving each other, just as God in Christ also has forgiven you" (Ephesians 4:31-32).

Why do you need to forgive? Does forgiving mean forgetting the offense? Does forgiving mean tolerating the offense? Does forgiving mean acknowledging the hurt? Does forgiving have any benefit for you, the injured party? Is it possible to forgive if the person who hurt you or your loved one is not alive or is unavailable?

9. "I in them and you in Me. May they be brought to complete unity to let the world know that you sent me and have loved them even as you have loved me" (John 17:23, NIV).

Jesus is praying to the Father for all believers in the above verse. Exactly how much does the Father love believers? Does this surprise you? Why would God the Father love believers to this degree? Tell yourself this astounding truth: God the Father loves (your name) as much as He loves Jesus.

10. "The Spirit Himself bears witness with our spirit that we are children of God, and if children, heirs also, heirs of God and fellow heirs with Christ" (Romans 8:16-17).

How does the Holy Spirit bear witness to your spirit that you are a child of God? What is an heir? What does an heir inherit? If we are fellow heirs with Jesus, what kind of inheritance will we receive?

# 9

## SET APART EXCLUSIVELY

This morning was going to be different. I decided to challenge myself to climb Camelback Mountain. And today was the day I was going to the top. Never mind if my knees knocked, arms ached, thighs throbbed, calves cried out, or my back bellowed. I was not going to listen to the complaints of those little pests. I had a single purpose in mind—the heights. After eating a fiber-filled, high energy, vitamin-laden breakfast of coffee and doughnuts (only kidding!), I began to dress for my big adventure. That took me an hour and a half. If I didn't make it to the top, at least I would look good! I usually hike in my jeans or sweats, but two things I always wear—my hiking boots and a hat.

My hiking boots are on the very top shelf in my closet. I guess it's a reminder that they take me to high places. They are big and heavy with wonderful gripping soles that enable me to climb with surefootedness. I only use my boots for hiking or climbing—nothing else. They have been set apart to take me to high places. Robert and I were invited to a wonderful black-tie ball recently, but I did not wear my hiking boots. Last Sunday as I got dressed for church, I did not reach for my hiking boots on the top shelf. Yesterday, I went to work out on the treadmill, but I did not lace up my hiking boots. They have been designed for special use, so they just don't go everywhere.

I was already breathing as though I had scaled the top of Mount Everest, yet all I had done was close my car door in the Echo Canyon parking lot. Anticipation can leave you breathless! The beginning of the trail is actually a series of steps carved into the earth and rock, by which the climber ascends very rapidly. It's a terrific aerobic exercise; after five steps up I had reached my target heart rate. All along the way I heard complaints. Knees, arms, calves, thighs, and back all had something to squawk about. But I would not listen. I was focused. I had one destination in mind and I would not quit.

There is one section of the trail that I just love. It has a handrail! I was disappointed at their lack of vision in not installing an escalator. The slope is about a 75° incline and is so steep in some places that many climbers find they need to use the handrail to pull themselves over the gigantic boulders. So it wasn't a "sissy" thing for me to do. My water bottle was getting a lot of use, and so were my wonderful hiking boots.

Halfway up the mountain was a real turning point for me. I lost my grip on a boulder and tried to plant my foot on some loose gravel. (I knew better than that.) But it was too late, and I began to slide down a group of small rocks. As I turned around so that I slid on my rear end, I sent up an impassioned "Peter prayer"—"Lord, save me!" I discovered that this was not a "walk in the park" for the uninitiated.

I tried to regain my composure and dignity as some smug mountain jogger ran by, asking if I was okay. "Oh I'm just fine. Just taking in the view." Prayer time! "Dear Father, I really need strength and perseverance for this. I had no idea how challenging this mountain was. Lord, do You know how discouraging it is to have these joggers run up the mountain? Oh that these hiking boots would make it to the summit—with me in them. Lord, take me farther than I ever thought I could go, not just up this mountain, but in my life. (I was beginning to see some spiritual significance in this climb.) I'm ready to scale the heights for You. (As I climbed higher, my commitment deepened.) I want to really live in the rarefied air of Your Presence as I have never done before, to use the gifts, talents, and abilities You have given me, for Your glory. I love You, Lord Jesus, and there isn't anything I wouldn't do for You. Take me farther than I ever thought I could go. Take me to the high places with You."

Do you have any idea how dangerous those kinds of prayers are? God thinks you're serious, and before you know it, He's taking you up on your promises! I know, because my God is a prayer-answering God.

Did I make it to the top of Camelback? Yes, I did! My achy breaky muscles pulled me up with one last pull, one last step, over one last boulder, and I was on the summit. All of Phoenix was spread out before me. I was elated, delighted, and happy as a clam at high water. Birds were actually soaring below me. God brought me to the high places with my boots on!

Sometimes we can hear God speak to us more clearly than at other times, and this was one of those clear times. It's not that the clouds opened up and I heard an audible voice, but I did hear Him. After all I was closer to the heavens than I had been all month. He said, "Roberta, I *will* take you farther than you ever thought you could go. I know the plans I have for you. Watch for my leading, be obedient, and walk in them." Do you know what I did that morning on the mountain? I consecrated myself to Jesus Christ. This was not the first time I had ever done that, but it was a fresh, new, heartfelt commitment. God, however, beat me to it. He set me apart for Himself long before I ever set myself apart for His purposes. But I was acknowledging what God tells all believers, "You, Child of God, are holy. You are set apart for Me, and I will take you to the high places."

## ANYONE HERE HOLY?

Holy. Is there anyone here who is "holy"? I posed that question to a group of women at one of my Bible studies. No one dared breathe, let alone reply! Holy? Are you kidding? Not me. Holy, now let me think. I'm sure St. Augustine, Mother Teresa, John Wesley, and Billy Graham are considered holy people. "What makes them holy?" I asked. There were many different answers, and before we started searching the Scriptures for evidence of "holy ones," we basically came to agree that these people had devoted their lives to serving God. They set themselves apart for God. And God set them apart for Himself. How would you answer if I asked you, "Are you holy?"

The definition of holy as given in the *Zondervan Encyclopedia of the Bible* is "sacred, sanctified, consecrated, to be set apart. No thing or person is holy in itself, but becomes holy as it is placed in relation to God."[1] Where have you placed yourself in relation to God? Just how far do you intend to go with Him? Farther than you ever thought you could go? Only one more step? Not an inch more? Only an observer? Just how "set apart" do you intend to live?

## IN SEARCH OF HOLINESS

Let me invite you to put on hiking boots and a hat and climb to the high places. There is a cave high in the mountains where solitude and stillness live. You've heard it rumored that this is where holiness can be found. You've always wanted to see what it looked like. So you and some of your friends decide to make the climb.

Before long as you ascend into the heights you find your backpack is far too heavy. Each of you searches your own pack for excess weight that is slowing your progress. In a little dark corner of your backpack you discover a book you had been reading. But you really wouldn't want your friends to see it, let alone have it accidentally drop out at the place where holiness is found. It's thick, heavy, dog-eared, and dirty, with some things in it that holy eyes were not meant to look upon. It's impeding your ascent to the high place of holiness. So you decide to throw it off the side of a sheer cliff. It's impossible to retrieve now. But where you're going there is no place for books about astrology, the occult, and explicit sexual encounters. You think, I'm really glad I got rid of that. And you recall a Scripture that you memorized: "...for his mouth speaks from that which fills his heart" (Luke 6:45c).

"If I fill my mind and heart with trash, that's what will come out of my mouth. Garbage in, garbage out." You return to digging around in your pack and find a bag of junk food filled with your favorite things— money, power, success, and material possessions. You vowed to save these only for emergencies, but it isn't the food that would really satisfy anyway. You've eaten from those tin cans before, and they always leave you empty with a bitter taste in your mouth. As you toss them out, the pack is definitely getting lighter.

Then you remember that little zippered pouch on the side. You say to yourself, "It's nothing really; it's only a little sin. Okay, so I've secretly cherished it, but it's not hurting anyone. That's one thing I'm not letting go of! Besides, it's my favorite sin." You took the leap a few years ago and invited Jesus into your heart, but perhaps inwardly you were hoping that you could keep a few favorite, secret sins. Now you're thinking, If I give Jesus an inch to work in my life, He'll take the whole mile! There's no telling what He'll ask me to do. Okay, okay, I'll throw my favorite sin on the trash heap. I know that Jesus probably won't stop until He's finished. I've heard He's like that. Another memorized verse comes to mind: "For I am confident of this very thing, that He who began a good work in you will perfect it until the day of Christ Jesus" (Philippians 1:6).

You think, Maybe I should reconsider this climb. There are several different trails along the way. I would have to choose the only one that goes straight up!

All of you are deep in thought as you decide to make camp for the night. As you fall asleep, you find yourself praying with your whole heart and soul, "Lord, I set myself apart for your glory, for your purposes. No longer will I hold on to those things that keep me from walking closely to You in the high places. So do with me as You will. Take me farther with You than I ever thought I could go. I'm ready." (Those dangerous prayers!)

The next morning everyone is quiet as the entrance to the cave comes into full view. Someone asks, "Before we enter the cave, we need to ask ourselves a question. Just how far in do we want to go?" Sally says, "Oh that's easy for me. Just far enough to say I've been there." She approaches it as though it were a tourist attraction: "I think I'll just take a few souvenirs from around the edges and return to lower ground."

You then realize that until last night you, too, were just a traveler, a bit of a tourist yourself, and full of conditions. You were setting limits on the journey, creating your own agenda, without risk or pain. But today it's different. You hear yourself say, "I'm ready to go farther than I ever thought I could go."

Only one person at a time can enter the cave, and you have to get on your knees to go through the low, small opening. You think, How appropriate. Breathlessly you go in and are astounded to find a clear, placid, mirrorlike pool. You sense you are about to behold the sacred. You lean over to gaze into the pool and see a clearly reflected image of yourself. You know the answer to the cave. You are looking at holiness, at perfection. This is the person God sees. You are a "Holy One." This is your identity. You are not the person seen in those distorted mirrors. You are not worthless, useless, and unimportant. God views you with "future perfect" eyes. He sees you as perfect and holy in Christ: "He has made perfect forever those who are being made holy" (Hebrews 10:14, NIV).

Max Lucado said it so well in his book *In The Eye of the Storm:* "Underline the word perfect. Note the word is not better. Not improving. Not on the upswing. God doesn't improve; He perfects. He doesn't enhance; He completes."[2]

Sally looked for holiness, too, but she only groped around the edges. She loved Jesus but didn't want to get carried away with all this enthusiasm about abandonment. She didn't mind the heavy backpack and never dumped anything out. Sally made her choice, and so must you. Some things are set aside for special purposes, like hiking boots and the holy ones they carry to the high places. How far you go depends on you.

## DIVINITY LIVES IN MY HOUSE

We are holy because Christ lives in us. Divinity lives in our house, our temple. "Or do you not know that your body is a temple of the Holy Spirit who is in you, whom you have from God, and that you are not your own? For you have been bought with a price: therefore glorify God in your body" (1 Corinthians 6:19-20).

We are a temple of God, a temple of the Holy Spirit, who dwells in us. Think of it as moving into a rented house. We don't really own it. It belongs to the Landlord. He reserves the right to inspect the property at any time. There are rules to abide by. We must dispose of any garbage, old rags, and rotting things at the request of the Landlord. This dwelling needs tender, loving care. If the windows need washing or something isn't working right, we need to bring it to the attention of the Landlord, even though He already knows. He can be quite demanding; He wants a very clean house. And He loves to hear from His tenants, especially since He shares the dwelling with us.

## THE REFINER'S FIRE

While on a trip to Johannesburg, South Africa, we visited a gold mine. I thought we'd walk around the grounds, see a few gold bars, and do lunch. So I wasn't too thrilled about stepping onto the elevator that descended hundreds of miles into the abyss. Okay, so maybe it wasn't hundreds, but it was a ticket for a journey to the center of the earth! I quickly realized it's no small effort to extract gold from the ore. Once the ore is brought to the surface, it is ground up, washed, and then refined. The refining process fascinated me the most. Plus I was above ground! I loved that part!

Gold is refined in a very hot furnace. Since gold melts at 1064.43°, we're talking hot! The furnace burns off all the impurities, waste matter, and rubbish. And the dross, which is the scum formed on the surface of the molten metal, is removed. The man working the furnace and pouring the molten gold into bars seemed to love his work. After the bars had cooled, he examined each one for imperfections, returning to the furnace any bars that were not pure enough. He said, "I must see my face clearly reflected in the gold bar."

How like God's refining fire! Have you ever had your dross removed? It's a never to be forgotten event! Unfortunately it's not a one-time affair. I'm sure God intended it to be that way. God is calling us to high and uncompromising standards. How far away our behavior is from His calling. We are "holy," but we are also in the process of being made holy. Sometimes God allows circumstances into our lives that will open the furnace doors to the refiner's fire. I've been there. You probably have as well. He allows the dross of our lives to be melted down and removed. Why? So that when He looks upon this "gold bar" He will see His image more clearly, His holy image. God does not allow us to go through suffering to tear us down, but to build us up. Because we are of such great worth, He refines us so that we will come forth as pure gold.

## FROM THE MOST POWERFUL MAN TO THE ALL-POWERFUL GOD

Going through the refiner's fire—being made holy—takes on many different forms. Charles W. Colson has been a soldier, statesman, lawyer, prisoner, and theologian. Colson served as special counsel to President Richard M. Nixon. Colson was a very powerful man who set his life apart for service to the most powerful man in the world—the president of the United States—and he was totally devoted to serving him. At times he winked at unethical behavior standards, and his ruthless manner earned him the dubious title of Nixon's "hatchet man." It was said of him, "Colson would walk over his own grandmother if he had to."

Colson's world as he had known it came to an abrupt halt when he pleaded guilty to charges related to the Watergate scandal of 1974. It was then he surrendered his life to the Lord. In his first real prayer he simply said, "I'm not much—the way I am now—but somehow I want to give myself to You. Take me."[3] Pride had been the spiritual cancer in his life up to that point. Now he would experience the humiliating life of a prisoner for seven grueling months. For him, a refiner's fire. Sometimes God has to set us apart from everything familiar and comfortable to enable us to be used by Him.

A true metamorphosis occurred in the life of Charles Colson. He has emerged on the other side as a man who has set his life apart for the glory of Jesus Christ. He now serves as chairman of Prison Fellowship, a Christian organization based in

Washington, D.C. Holy people come in all shapes and sizes. Here was a life that had been dedicated to serving the most powerful man in the world, which only brought him grief and despair. Now he serves the all-powerful God of the universe, who gives him peace and hope. What we set ourselves apart for makes all the difference!

## AN ORDINARY WOMAN DOING THE EXTRAORDINARY

Through the ages there have been thousands upon thousands of people who have chosen to glorify God with their lives and who have set themselves apart for Christ. One of these is a poor, ordinary woman who has done extraordinary things.

Mother Teresa is a slightly built nun who lives and works in the streets of Calcutta. She is not particularly clever or savvy in the art of persuasion, but that is not especially important in her work. She is recognized worldwide for her devotion to the poorest of the poor. Does she seem distant to us? Too difficult to identify with? Actually she was really quite average until she set about to do something most exceptional. In 1949 as she was establishing the Missionaries of Charity, her small band of women, she said, "They were my students. They wanted to give everything to God, and they were in a hurry to do it. They took off their expensive saris with great satisfaction in order to put on our humble cotton ones. They came, fully aware of the difficulties. When a girl who belongs to a very old caste comes to place herself at the service of the outcasts, we are talking about a revolution, the biggest one, the hardest of all: the revolution of love!"

These young women set aside the prized status of their Indian culture to take a monumental step. As one by one they came, Mother Teresa prayed for them, "Father, I pray for them that they may be dedicated to your holy name, sanctified to You, reserved for Your service. To this end I consecrate myself to You."[4]

They are dedicated to rescue the derelict left to die in the streets—the starving, abandoned child and the leper with his twisted limbs and sightless eyes. Who are these women? How would they describe themselves? They are the hands and feet, the voice and heart of Jesus Christ—holy women who set themselves apart to be used by God. To most of us the streets of Calcutta are light-years away. We serve in a different arena. But are we really so dissimilar? We too are the hands and feet, the voice and heart of Jesus. We work in shops, airports, offices, hospitals, and homes. We are no less holy in these places. How we set our lives apart and share Jesus with others is what makes an ordinary person, like you or me, extraordinary—"holy."

## WE ARE THE BRIDE OF CHRIST

Have you ever noticed how busy Christians are in their holy journey? We walk with faith, run with endurance, shout with joy, clap our hands, fight the good fight, entertain angels, preach the Word, do battle with the enemy, and wait patiently for the Lord. Wait a minute! Waiting patiently doesn't take movement, does it? Yes it does. It is in the waiting that we grow in ways that walking and running will never produce. Waiting creates a balanced life. Waiting is another way we set ourselves apart for Christ. We are all waiting expectantly for our Bridegroom to come for us. It is in the waiting that we are preparing for Him. We are being made holy in the process.

Believers have a unique and special relationship with Jesus Christ. It's very much like a bride who has been set apart exclusively for her bridegroom. We have made a commitment to Jesus, and now we belong to Him.

The Scriptures regard the Church, which includes all believers in Christ, as the "Bride of Christ." It's much easier for women to grasp this concept and truth because we either have been, are preparing to be, or possibly one day hope to be a bride. It is a time of great significance in one's life, when both men and women have chosen just one person to commit themselves to. They set themselves apart for just one.

By examining the Jewish marriage customs in biblical times, we can gain a whole new understanding of our identity in Christ and can better grasp the significance of the biblical promises of Jesus. The very first step in a Jewish marriage was betrothal. The bridegroom would leave his father's house and travel to the home of his prospective bride. There the bridegroom would pay the purchase price, and the marriage covenant was established. From that time on the bride was said to be consecrated or sanctified, set apart exclusively for her bridegroom. As a symbol of the covenant relationship, the couple would drink a cup of wine that had been blessed.

The groom would then return alone to the home of his father where he would prepare a place in his father's house for his bride to live with him. When the accommodations were ready and the period of separation was over, the groom would come for his bride. He usually came at night, accompanied by his best man and other companions in a torchlight procession to the bride's home. Although the bride knew he was coming, she didn't know exactly when, so she would wait expectantly. When the groom was just a short distance from the bride's home, he would announce his arrival with a shout to alert his bride to be prepared for his coming. The wedding party would then return to the home of the groom's father where they would greet all the wedding guests gathered for the wedding feast.[5]

To us this may sound like a quaint and charming marriage custom, but Jesus drew a strong analogy from the Jewish marriage customs of His time so that His followers would better grasp what He promised. "In My Father's house are many dwelling places; if it were not so, I would have told you; for I go to prepare a place for you. And if I go and prepare a place for you, I will come again, and receive you to Myself; that where I am, there you may be also" (John 14:2-3).

Just as the Jewish bridegroom left his father's house to travel to his prospective bride's home, so Jesus left His heavenly home with His Father to come to earth to be with His prospective Bride, the Church. The Jewish bridegroom paid a price to purchase his bride. Jesus paid for us, His Bride, with His own life, so we belong to Him. As the Scripture says, "Do you not know that...you are not your own? For you have been bought with a price: therefore glorify God in your body" (1 Corinthians 6:19-20).

As the Jewish groom shared the wine with his bride, he established a covenant relationship with her and gave his life to her. Jesus also established a covenant the night he instituted communion as He shared the cup of wine with His disciples and later spilled his blood. "This cup is the new covenant in My blood" (1 Corinthians 11:25b).

After the covenant was established, the Jewish bride was then said to be sanctified or set apart exclusively for her groom. So we also as the "Bride of Christ" are set apart exclusively for Christ. "We have been sanctified through the offering of the body of Jesus Christ once for all" (Hebrews 10:10).

The Jewish bridegroom then returned to his father's house to prepare a place for his bride. After Jesus died and rose from the dead, He ascended into heaven and returned to His Father's house to prepare a place for us.

The Jewish bride expects her groom but does not know the exact time of his arrival. So she must be prepared for Him at all times. We, also, must be prepared at all times for Jesus' promised return: "Therefore be on the alert, for you do not know which day your Lord is coming" (Matthew 24:42).

As the Jewish groom came back for his bride, so will Jesus come back for us. He will descend from heaven with a shout, just like the Jewish bridegroom announcing his arrival. "For the Lord Himself will descend from heaven with a shout..." (1 Thessalonians 4:16).

We will be taken to the Father's house in heaven, just as the Jewish bride was taken to the home of her bridegroom's father. Think about it. Jesus created this unbelievably magnificent world in just six days. And He has been preparing a new place for us for almost two thousand years! It's going to be spectacular! Like the Jewish bride and groom arriving at the father's house to be greeted by all the wedding guests waiting for them, so one day we will be greeted by the assembly of believers at the heavenly wedding feast.

Isn't this a beautiful analogy? Do you see what it says to us today? This world is not all there is. Our lives are set apart for a high purpose—here on earth and then in heaven. Our identity is that of a bride that

Jesus presents as pure and blameless to the Father. This is a time of preparation until the Bridegroom comes for us.

And just as it was possible in biblical times during the separation while the bridegroom was preparing a place for his bride that she could commit adultery, so we also may jeopardize our relationship with Christ by being unfaithful to Him: "You adulteresses, do you not know that friendship with the world is hostility toward God? Therefore whoever wishes to be a friend of the world makes himself an enemy of God" (James 4:4).

It's time to quit playing games and get serious about sin. We cannot be in love with the godless world system and in love with Jesus at the same time. Be on the alert and be prepared. Our Bridegroom may come with a shout at any moment. He will come as a Beloved Thief in the night and snatch His Bride away to be with Him forever. How God has honored us! He is devoted to our character, our holiness, our purity, and our future with Him. We are not a downtrodden people struggling through life searching for identity and purpose. We belong to Christ, and He is committed to perfect us in Him. May the fire of the Holy Spirit burn this truth in our hearts!

## LOVE NOTE TO GOD

I'm holy, I'm really holy! Father, I had no idea how important it was for me to know this identity You've given me. You have stirred within me the desire to live my life with the continual thought that I am set apart for You. Teach me not to waste my sufferings but to see them as the refining process that I might come forth as pure gold. Thank you for Your Holy Spirit who will enable and empower me to prepare for the coming of my Bridegroom.

Love,
Me

## TELLING YOURSELF THE TRUTH

1. Have you ever been challenged to go further in something than you thought you could go? Describe what happened. How did you feel when it was over? Did you feel better able to take on another, perhaps even greater, challenge as a result of this experience?

2. What does the identity "holy" mean to you personally? What living person would you describe as "holy"? What is it about that person that makes him or her different?

3. "He has made perfect forever those who are being made holy" (Hebrews 10:14, NIV).

How can we be made perfect? Can we make ourselves "more" perfect for God? The Father sees us as perfect in Christ. What does that mean to you?

4. Have you ever prayed a "dangerous" prayer like, "There isn't anything I wouldn't do for you, Lord"? What happened as a result? If you prayed a "dangerous" prayer, what might you say? What keeps you from saying that?

5. Have you had a favorite sin that was tough to let go of? Did you ever make a decision to throw it in the trash heap? Have you ever gone back searching

through the garbage to retrieve it? Did you ever ask anyone to pray for you in this matter? Why not ask a friend to pray for you never to go back to that sin? You don't have to give details about the sin; just identify it as sin.

6. "For his mouth speaks from that which fills his heart" (Luke 6 45c).

Name the various ways information fills our minds and hearts. Which of these has the greatest impact on your thoughts and speech? If you do not control what you see, hear, and read, what kind of views, values, and vocabulary will fill your mind? With what good and profitable things can you fill your mind?

7. "Or do you not know that your body is a temple of the Holy Spirit who is in you, whom you have from God, and that you are not your own? For you have been bought with a price: therefore glorify God in your body" (1 Corinthians 6:19-20).

God created the body with natural appetites. Can we satisfy our sexual needs as we do our need of food? Today's society advocates "If it feels good, do it." What message does this send about the worth of a human being? What is the worth of a person in God's eyes? Which do you think is the most accurate? Society's opinion or God's? What practical ways can you glorify God in your body?

8. "You adulteresses, do you not know that friendship with the world is hostility toward God? Therefore whoever wishes to be a friend of the world makes himself an enemy of God" (James 4:4).

One of the definitions of "friend" in *Webster's New World Dictionary* is "A person on the same side in a struggle." Why can't we be friends with the world and friends with God? How might we be friends of the world and an enemy of God? Why do you think the word "adulteresses" was used? What does this assume about a believer's relationship with Christ?

9. "We have been sanctified through the offering of the body of Jesus Christ once for all" (Hebrew 10:10).

The word sanctify means to set apart as holy. Is it possible for believers to sanctify themselves? If so, to what extent? How has God sanctified believers? Why would He do this?

10. List the identities and names that you have learned so far. Which is the most meaningful to you? Why? How do you practically live this out?

# 10

## DIFFERENCE MAKERS

They were born to a cocaine-addicted mother who was a prostitute. The place these two beautiful young children called home was a crack house for drug users. There they ate stale, rotten food, if any, slept on the floor, played games, and lived their tender, fragile lives. Swaggering strangers looking for sex and drugs stumbled into the house at all hours of the night, disturbing the children's sleep as they lay on filthy, moth-eaten mattresses. The air was continually smoke filled and stagnant with the ever present stench of urine. When the children were found, there was no food in the house for the four-year-old girl and six-year-old boy, the boy allegedly had been sexually abused, and the mother had just given birth to her third child.

What kind of life would these children have? What hopes and dreams would never be realized? What opportunities would open up to them? Who would ever hear the cries of help from their confused and frightened hearts? Who would ever speak for the best interests of these abused and neglected children?

One of the answers to these questions is my dear friend Kathy, a CASA (Court Appointed Special Advocate) volunteer. A CASA worker is a trained community volunteer who is appointed by a juvenile court judge to speak for children who are brought before the court. Children such as these frequently become victims again, this time of an overburdened juvenile justice system where there are too many cases within too little time, and with too few resources available to give to each child. Far too often the child slips farther and farther through the cracks, and wounds get deeper and deeper. The child never feels that he or she is worthwhile as a person, is loved, or is listened to. But my friend Kathy is a "Difference Maker," and she listened. As a result, the children in this story have now been placed in an adoptive home with loving, committed caretakers. They are taking piano lessons, going to school, and living lives filled with hope and a future.

You may remember Kathy as the person who took that "challenging" typing class with me. "Now I know why I had to take that class," she says. "My court reports to the judges must be typed. See, God prepares us before He sends us out." Kathy commits each case to prayer before the Lord. She lives her life steeped in biblical principles although she works in a secular environment. The people she works with may never hear a Bible verse quoted from Kathy's lips, but they will see the life of Christ in her actions, her concern, and her love. She's a living Bible!

Since we are the best of friends, we have spent much time over the years in prayer for one another. We commit our plans and our dreams into the hands of the Lord to do as He sees fit with our lives. Kathy used to say, "God has given me a real desire to work with needy children. I don't know what I'm supposed to do or where I'm to do it, but I want to be available to be used by God." Notice the key word *available*. "Difference Makers" are available to be used by God, and because Kathy was "available," God has used her to bring hope and a better life to dozens of children.

## THE LIGHT OF THE WORLD

"You are the light of the world. Let your light shine before men in such a way that they may see your good works, and glorify your Father who is in heaven" (Matthew 5:14a, 16).

A "Difference Maker," as I have defined it here, is a believer who changes things in a positive way as a result of being "light" in the world. Such people reflect, renew, remake, reshape, rebuild, revive, reveal, reform, realign, re-create, redesign, and restructure. They illumine, enlighten, ignite, and inform. The "Light of the World" is not invisible! "A city on a hill cannot be hidden. Neither do people light a lamp and put it under a bowl. Instead they put it on its stand, and it gives light to everyone in the house" (Matthew 5:14b-15, NIV).

You, believer, are the "Light of the World," and your presence makes a "difference." God calls us to make a difference for Christ in this sin-sick and dying world. In the places where we live and work our influence should be felt. When we walk into the dark places of life, our presence ought to dispel the darkness. We are the "Light of the World," and God uses light in His work, such as reaching out to one in need, loving the unlovely, rescuing the helpless, and sharing the gospel of Jesus Christ by our illuminating example. We are incredibly important to the purposes of God!

## A HUNGRY MAN OF WORTH

When I consider "Difference Makers" who are indeed living as the "Light of the World," Anne Marie Ritchie comes to mind. Anne Marie and her husband, Ron, and some friends decided to spend the day at Fisherman's Wharf in San Francisco. They spread out their blanket on a grassy area overlooking the bay and laid out a splendid lunch of fresh crab and sourdough bread. They were cracking the shells and bit by bit, piece by piece, removing the crab from its home. Fresh crab by the bay, good friends, good fellowship—all was well with the world.

Except what Anne Marie's keen eyes picked up on. A street person was watching them. A lonely spectator, he listened to their laughter and hungrily eyed their luncheon fare. Edging his way closer and closer, he soon became impossible to ignore. He was about twenty-eight years old, rather sickly looking, and definitely hungry. The foul odor surrounding the man was indeed the most repulsive smell that ever offended nostrils.

Now Ron is a pastor and a man who passionately seeks after God's heart, but he is also human. He lifted his eyes toward heaven and sighed a silent prayer to the Lord, "Oh no, Lord, please. It's my day off."

But Anne Marie, her hands filled with crab and her mouth tasting the sweet morsels of meat, was moved to pity. She greeted him, "Good day. Would you like to join us?"

He shook his head.

"Are you hungry?" she asked.

He nodded.

Anne Marie then broke off a section of the crab shell and some sourdough bread and handed them to him.

Then she saw his hands and gasped. The threadbare gloves were shredded and sparsely covered his crippled and gnarled fingers. "I can't eat it," he said.

"Then sit down with me." Anne Marie bit by bit, piece by piece, fed him her lunch with her own strong, sure hands. She broke the crab and bread into bite-sized pieces, lifted them to his lips, and fed the hungry stranger as she said, "I'm doing this in the name of Jesus Christ." The small gathering of people on the blanket was hushed as it witnessed a beautiful, moving sight. This woman saw this man as God created him, a man of worth. A man Jesus shed his blood for.

Anne Marie is a "Difference Maker," a "Light of the World," one who is dear to my heart. Early in my Christian life she was the one who first told me of my identity in Christ. She said, "Roberta, you are a 'Daughter of the King.'" I'd never heard such a thing before! I treasured that knowledge. How I desired to learn all I could about how a "Daughter of the King" ought to live. This book is a direct result of that first seed of my identity in Christ that was planted by this precious woman. Anne Marie has made a difference in my life from that day forward. Just as she did with that hungry stranger, she gave me a sense of dignity and worth. This is how "Difference Makers" are to live.

## SALT OF THE EARTH

"You are the salt of the earth; but if the salt has become tasteless, how will it be made salty again? It is good for nothing anymore, except to be thrown out and trampled under foot by men" (Matthew 5:13).

Salt is a purifying and preserving agent. In biblical times in the Roman world it symbolized purity. Jesus described believers as "salt" to demonstrate the influence of their lives in preserving and bringing purity into the world. Because of its medicinal qualities, newborn babies were bathed in it and rubbed with it. Salt was also used as a form of money. Due to its great value as a basic staple of life, Roman soldiers were frequently paid with salt. That is the basis for the word "salary."

As flavoring, salt is sprinkled over the food. If it is dumped all on one spot, the food becomes absolutely inedible. We as believers are to be spread abroad into society, as opposed to being lumped together in our "holy huddles." We are called to be a force, not a fortress. In the act of sprinkling, the salt loses itself in what it is to flavor. It's not the salt one tastes, but the effects of it. You and I as believers in the world are to sprinkle ourselves about so that the effects on society are to flavor, preserve, purify, create thirst, and melt the ice of hard hearts.

What does this suggest to you? How can you practically make a difference in your world? One of the ways I strive to make a difference is with my everyday tasks and events. Whenever I get my nails or hair done, I always pray for the individual working on me. There is a unique closeness with these special people who do services like this for us. As believers we should be aware of the wonderful opportunities for "sprinkling salt" that these times afford us.

One day my nails needed work badly, and I decided to go to a new, lovely, young nail technician. Brenda had been highly recommended to me by several people. (And God had a plan!) During the course of the manicure, I asked my usual questions about her life, interests, and family. Then I put my "salt shaker" on the table, right? Wrong! Salt was meant to be sprinkled around, not left in its container. It was easy and natural for me to talk about God as she asked me what I did. Brenda responded with, "You don't look like a Bible teacher." (Could have been the sweats, Reeboks, and sequined baseball cap I wore.)

Then I tried to test her spiritual temperature. I dropped a few words, without really quoting any verses, about the greatest book (the Bible) I'd ever read. I was conscious of "creating thirst" just in case she was looking for the Giver of Living Water. Salt does that. I thought, Is she sincerely interested in spiritual things? Is she searching with her heart? Or is she just a collector of spiritual knowledge, searching only with her mind? Brenda didn't give me a clue as to where she was on her spiritual journey, but I silently prayed for her as she worked on my hands and we chatted.

I went to Brenda for a number of months and continued praying for her and her husband, but there was still no discernible interest in God. At least I didn't perceive any. But God was working in her heart. One day as I walked in the salon, Brenda's face was somehow brighter, different, and more transparent. "Roberta," she said, "I have found God!" This was music to my ears, and I wanted to hear more about my favorite subject. The evangelist in me was surfacing again.

"Brenda, how did this happen? What led to this decision? What exactly have you done?" I discovered that Brenda had a spiritual awakening but had not made a decision for Jesus. She asked me some probing questions about Jesus and was getting very "thirsty." So I began to present the gospel to her.

As the second coat of polish was being applied, I became aware of the woman sitting beside us who was Brenda's next appointment. Jane was listening intently. I didn't have much time; my polish was drying! I raised my voice a bit. The gospel is such good news, she needed to catch every word too! Before long Jane joined in the conversation. I looked around and thought, Wow, we're on a roll, Lord! Anyone else here thirsty? The results? Jane and her sister came to my home for a Christmas luncheon where I presented the gospel to a houseful of women. Both Jane and her sister came to know Jesus and now attend a Bible study. Brenda also committed her life to Jesus, and her husband followed with a decision for Christ about two months later.

We, as Christians, are the "Salt of the Earth." This is who we are in Christ. This is our name, our true identity. Ah, but to live as the salt of the earth is another story, isn't it? It means living on the edge. For some of us, living on the edge means hanging our feet over the edge of our private swimming pool! Having such an identity requires responsibility. Salt loses its taste in salt cellars, you know. So it is with us if we keep all our salt in our personal shaker at home and never sprinkle it anywhere.

Tim Hansel gives a wonderful illustration about what happens to "salt" when it isn't used.

He saw people love each other....And he saw that all love made strenuous demands on the lovers. He saw love required sacrifice and self-denial. He saw love produce arguments and anguish....And he decided that it cost too much. And he decided not to diminish his life with love.

He saw people strive for distant and hazy goals. He saw men strive for success...women strive for high, high, ideals...and he saw that the striving was frequently mixed with disappointment. And he saw the strong men fail....He saw it force people into pettiness....He saw that those who succeeded were sometimes those who had not earned the success. And he decided that it cost too much. He decided not to soil his life with striving.

He saw people serving others. He saw men give money to the poor and helpless....And he saw that the more they served, the faster the need grew....He saw ungrateful receivers turn on their serving friends....He decided not to soil his life with serving.

And when he died, he walked up to God and presented Him with his life. Undiminished, unmarred, and unsoiled, his life was clean from the filth of the world, and he presented it proudly...saying, "This is my life."

And the great God said, "What life?"[1]

In biblical times salt that had lost its saltiness was applied as manure to the soil. It was also used to hasten the decomposition of dung.[2] Not a pretty picture. You may not share the gospel in the manner that I do—after all not everyone wants to wear sequined baseball caps—but what is important is that you sprinkle salt in your community in your own way, as Joanne Everitt does.

## CALLED TO MAKE AN IMPACT

Joanne Everitt committed her life to Jesus Christ at age twenty-six. She quickly began to understand that God had a high purpose for her (just as He has for all of us). For the first time her life had meaning, and she was ready to be radical for Christ. As Joanne studied the Bible, she learned about the dramatic role Christians are called to play in the world. Joanne and her husband David felt called to make an impact on society for Christ, so they became politically involved. They saw a real need to inform the Christian community of the affairs of government. The Everitts set up a program to present in churches called the *Watchman Program*. As Dave gave an informational talk about our legislators and the political process, Joanne set up a table at the back of the church and registered people to vote.

While attending a national affairs briefing in Dallas, Texas, they first came face to face with the abortion issue through the film *Assignment Life*. Joanne said, "We simply weren't the same after that movie." They knew it was God's design to protect and preserve preborn babies, but what could be done for women in a crisis pregnancy? It wasn't enough to offer information and alternatives to abortion. Free services and goods were needed, such as counseling, childbirth and prenatal classes, maternity clothes and baby items, adoption information, support groups, and parenting classes. The needs were so great for these women as they faced perhaps the greatest personal crisis of their lives. What difference could two people make?

Joanne and David were led to set up the Crisis Pregnancy Centers of Greater Phoenix, where they offer free all those needed services, as well as many others. In their first year they handled 336 cases. In 1992 in one month alone they had 400 cases. Joanne found the perfect place where God had called her to serve and to be "salt."

Joanne says, "You win every time you educate. It's the responsibility of the church to speak the truth, and it's the Holy Spirit's job to convict the world." Joanne does just that as she faces the TV cameras and news media as a spokesperson for crisis pregnancies and the precious lives involved. There is help, there is concern, and there is understanding for the special needs of women in crisis pregnancies because of Joanne and Dave Everitt. How fortunate for all the lives rescued as a result of their commitment to making a difference for God. Of those people it can truly be said, "They are the 'Salt of the Earth.'"

Perhaps you are not called to serve in such a high profile capacity, but you, Christian, are called to serve. Whatever your task, it is no less important. Whatever your gifts, talents, or abilities, they are no less effective. God planned your unique life from ages past. Now all of the hosts of heaven are watching and waiting to see you, the "Salt of the Earth," live a decidedly radical life for Christ. Does that sound strange to you? You say you have never done a radical thing in your life? Take a long hard look at the God you serve and are called to follow. Jesus Christ was the most unpredictable, amazing, disturbing, astonishing, awesome, radical person that ever walked the face of this earth! This is no boring, humdrum, weak-willed, out of touch, indecisive, ineffective Master you serve. Deciding to make a radical difference for Christ could be the most momentous day in your life. Surely all of heaven will rejoice.

## FRAGRANCE OF CHRIST

"For we are a fragrance of Christ to God among those who are being saved and among those who are perishing; to the one an aroma from death to death, to the other an aroma from life to life" (2 Corinthians 2:15-16).

History is filled with great men and women of God who made a difference as a result of radical lives committed to Jesus Christ. Actually they were ordinary men and women like you and me. They just chose to live extraordinary lives. Mary the sister of Martha and Lazarus was such a person.

Jesus was the honored guest in the home of Mary, Martha, and Lazarus in Bethany just six days before the Passover. Jesus was well aware that this would be the last time He would be with His close friends. His passion and death were imminent. Perhaps they also sensed it in their hearts. It was so much like a farewell feast, especially for Mary. Perhaps Mary had planned this for some time, or maybe the thought came to her as she sat listening at the Master's feet, which she did often. But this evening she rose and left the room for a moment.

Jesus was reclining at the table when Mary entered again with an alabaster jar of expensive perfume in her hands. All eyes were upon her as she broke the seal on the vial of perfume. Those sitting close-by caught a bit of the fragrance as it escaped from the jar and dissipated into the air. She knelt down before the

Master and began to pour the costly perfume over His feet. The perfume spilled out, flowed over, and anointed His feet. She adored her Lord and desired to unabashedly display her total devotion to Him. It was an extravagant, expensive expression of love for Jesus. Mary had anointed the Anointed One. Soon Jesus would pour forth His life and spill out His blood in an extravagant, expensive expression of love for you and me.

Although it was unthinkable for a woman to let down her hair in public, Mary unbound her long tresses of rich dark hair and let them fall over the feet of Jesus. She then gathered her hair in her hands and reverently and tenderly dried His feet with it. The fragrance was absorbed into her glistening hair. Mary had recklessly abandoned herself in uninhibited devotion to her Lord, in a selfless act of total surrender and submission. It was a holy, silent, breathless moment. The exquisite fragrance enveloped the room and then filled the house. It began to spill out the windows into the evening air, the garden beyond, down the road, and on through the centuries until even today at this moment as your eyes gaze upon these words, Mary is remembered for her outpouring of lavish love for Jesus. And the fragrance is still in the air!

Think about it for a moment. Mary's hair held the fragrance of the perfume as a wonderful reminder that she had given her love in total abandonment to the Master. For many days after that special evening, wherever Mary walked, the fragrance filled the air. As she fell asleep upon her bed that night, as she rose the following morning, as she met with her friends and went to the market and the synagogue, the fragrance still present in her hair reminded her that she had been with Jesus. Surely others noticed and commented on that lovely perfume.

## MY FAVORITE PERFUME

As believers we are the "Fragrance of Christ." We are the fragrance of His knowledge in every place. We bear the unmistakable mark of "having been with Jesus" and influencing the world as a result. It *will* be noticed. Others *will* comment.

The other day my daughter Shannon was in my bathroom and sprayed on my favorite perfume. It was at least an hour later when I entered my bathroom, yet I could still smell the fragrance. I was very aware that she had been in that room. That's how it is to be with believers such as you and me. We are to have such an impact on society that we are remembered for the "fragrance" we carried. It should still be present long after we've gone.

We are to be a "Fragrance of Christ" among those who are being saved. They love to be around us. And why not? We wear their favorite perfume! We impact their lives. They hear words of truth, encouragement, hope, and life from our lips. We are also a "Fragrance of Christ" among those who are perishing. They absolutely hate that "fragrance" we stubbornly insist on wearing. They back off from our presence every chance they get. We impact their lives and they want no part of it. They are dying spiritually. They prefer perishing and wouldn't have it any other way. Know anyone like that? The last thing they want to hear are words of life and truth. Some will reject the "fragrance."

Let's return to that amazing anointed scene in Bethany two thousand years ago. Suddenly and harshly the peace of that evening was broken by the caustic criticism of Judas Iscariot: "'Why was this perfume not sold for three hundred denarii, and given to poor people?' Now he said this, not because he was concerned about the poor, but because he was a thief, and as he had the money box, he used to pilfer what was put into it" (John 12:5-6).

How could Judas be so calculating and judgmental after just witnessing Mary's total outpouring of love for Jesus? Did he not breathe in the fragrance also? Was he not moved? Judas shared in Jesus' life for almost three years. He saw Him heal the sick, raise the dead, forgive sinners, and reach deep within the souls of men and women. Jesus came to Mary's defense, "Let her alone....For the poor you always have with you, but you do not always have Me" (John 12:7a, 8). Judas did not care for the poor; he cared only for his own selfish desires. How could Judas have lived and walked with Jesus, yet be so insensitive and without understanding? Today it is no different.

Check out the people who fill the pews in our churches. Some of them say all the Christian buzzwords, sing in the choir, give to the missions, and even serve on the boards, but their hearts are far from God. We, however, are called to be different. We are who we are because Jesus Christ lives in us. His Holy Spirit enables us and empowers us. It is the work of God in us.

## SHINE LIKE STARS

As believers, we are God's hands, feet, mouth, and eyes. We can see the needy with compassionate eyes. We can feed the hungry with our own strong, sure hands. We are given the privilege to speak words of hope, truth, worth, and dignity to those who have been told they are hopeless, worthless, and expendable. We have been entrusted with the words of life, to share the truth, the gospel of Jesus Christ with this corrupt and needy world. When the gospel is rejected, we need to remind ourselves that they are not rejecting us, but Christ. We have been given a high calling of privilege and responsibility, honor and duty. Our worth comes from our identity in Christ, not from the world's ever-changing opinion of us. The most trustworthy opinion is the me God sees. We are to "shine like stars in the universe as you hold out the word of life..." (Philippians 2:15b-16a, NIV).

We can make an incredible difference in our world! We are to shine like stars in the universe as we reflect the pure light that comes from our Heavenly Source. We are a "Fragrance of Christ," the "Light of the World," and "Salt of the Earth." We do indeed impact the world in a mighty way! Heaven is all on tiptoes peering over the edge watching us expectantly with great delight. It sees "Difference Makers" at work!

## LOVE NOTE TO GOD

Dear Father, You have put such a high calling on my life. How could I ever attain it without Your Holy Spirit? I am grateful that You have given me a purpose, a destiny, abilities, talents, and gifts. Reveal to me the paths You would have me walk, the people You would have me impact, the work You would have me do. Just like the alabaster jar, I'm ready to be spilled out and broken for You.

Love,
Me

# TELLING YOURSELF THE TRUTH

1. Have you ever made a practical difference in someone's life? An infant's? A teenager's? An unwed mother's? An invalid's? An elderly person's? What were the circumstances? How did you make a difference? How did you feel about yourself afterwards?

2. Has anyone ever been a "Difference Maker" in your life? Who was it? What were the circumstances? How did you feel about yourself afterwards? How did you feel about the "Difference Maker"? Have you ever acknowledged your gratefulness to that person? In what way?

3. If you could make a significant difference in anyone's life, who would it be? What would you do? What results would you hope to accomplish?

4. "You are the light of the world. A city on a hill cannot be hidden. Neither do people light a lamp and put it under a bowl. Instead they put it on its stand, and it gives light to everyone in the house. In the same way, let your light shine before men, that they may see your good deeds and praise your Father in heaven" (Matthew 5:14-16, NIV).

How would you define "light of the world" as it is used in these verses? Does this verse mean that you should display your good works for all to see? Could this be an opportunity for pride? How should your light shine?

5. Rewrite Romans 12:3 in your own words: "...not

to think more highly of himself than he ought to think; but to think so as to have sound judgment..."

If you are not to think more highly of yourself, then is it good for you to think less of yourself? What does it mean to "think so as to have sound judgment"?

6. Define *pride* and *humility*, using a dictionary. Is it permissible to be proud of one's accomplishments? How does that differ from prideful arrogance?

7. How would you explain "light" to a blind friend? In what ways can a believer be "the light of the world"?

8. List all the uses for regular salt you can think of. Apply at least three of them to the life of a believer. How have you personally "lived out" one of these?

9. "For we are a fragrance of Christ to God..." (2 Corinthians 2:15).

Have you ever been around people who were the "Fragrance of Christ"? What were they like? How did they live? How did they affect you? What do you think is God's favorite fragrance? What emotion does that evoke in you?

10. How have you been challenged by this chapter? What are you going to do about it? Share your decisions with your group. Or write them down in a journal and date them. Decide to make a difference for Christ in this needy world.

# 11

TELLING YOURSELF THE TRUTH

Finally we were going into the vaults! I had been looking forward to this day for many months. As part of the docent training program for the Phoenix Art Museum, I had the rare privilege of seeing what few are able to set their eyes upon. Our class was escorted through many closed doors and much security deep into the bowels of the museum. Here we would view how treasured works of art were stored in between times of exhibition. Each piece had been carefully catalogued and assigned to its designated holding-place until it was selected to be displayed. Paintings were hung on special, sliding, wire racks to guard them from brushing up against one another. Sculptures were on shelves lined with carpeting so they wouldn't be damaged upon removal. Fragile porcelain bowls were stored upside down to protect the pieces from tipping over. A great deal of time and attention had gone into the storing of these important works of art.

What do you imagine these museum treasures think about their predicament? "I am supposed to be a masterpiece created by a recognized artist. Big deal!

Here I sit in some climate-controlled basement storage away from the limelight until one of the bespectacled curators finally decides to put me to work. Obviously I'm not worth much if I can't prove it to the world."

Of course we would say, "Ridiculous." First to animated paintings, second to the idea of worthlessness. But that is exactly what we do. We evaluate ourselves based on performance. We tend to think that what we do is more important than who we are. Few would question the value of the treasures in the museum vaults. Many of them are priceless. Special care has been given to them while they are in storage. It's not whether they are put on display that determines their worth. They are valuable no matter where they are or how they are being used.

Believers often are discontent like the museum's masterpieces in the vaults. That's not God's idea. Our worth is not in what we do but in who we are. Who we are determines what we do. We are in Christ! The lies we tell ourselves muddy up our minds.

## FOOLISH BELIEFS

So what is the truth? Some people actually accept the following beliefs as true. I even believed the ones about Homer and Portia until I was enlightened!

Glasnost is a streak-free window cleaner.
An Ionic column is on the editorial page.
The "Gettysburg Address" is where Lincoln lived.
The London Underground is a political movement.
Plato is a planet. Plato is a dog.
Homer swung a mean baseball bat.
Portia is a red-hot sports car.
New Guinea is at the local pet store.

Paul Revere cried out, "Every man for himself."
Megabytes are treated by orthodontists.
Software is a nightgown.
Guerrilla warfare is a food fight at the zoo!

Some of the things we have believed about our identity must sound just as foolish to God.

## THE LIES WE BELIEVE

"I'm a homemaker. I volunteer at the hospital twice a week, take a French class, play in a tennis league, lead a weekly Bible study, carpool our two children, and serve on the Women's Ministry Board at church. With all I'm doing I must be a woman of worth, but I'm so depressed, to say nothing of being exhausted." The lie? Performance equals worth.

"I try to please everyone in my life. Their love and approval is all I'm looking for. I'll do anything so that people will like me. I just don't feel worthwhile unless I'm accepted by everyone, but it's making me crazy." The lie? I need the approval of everyone to feel valuable.

"I'm very successful in my career. My salary is in the six digits. I'm most definitely an overachiever in all I do. A great deal of praise and admiration come my way, but it's never good enough for me. In my effort to be 'the best,' I'm never satisfied with just doing 'my best.' I feel so defeated." The lie? I must be perfect to earn approval.

"I am very conscious of looking fit. Fat, sugar, and red meat simply are not part of my vocabulary, much less my diet. I jog, bike, swim, and lift weights to stay in shape. After a Hawaiian vacation of eating and lying on the beach I gained five pounds. I'm disgusted with myself. My self-worth depends on my size six dress and what the scale says every morning." The lie? I must look perfect to feel good about myself.

"I haven't made a sale in months. I'm miserable. I'm depressed. I feel I'm only as good as what I do. Never mind character or integrity. The bottom line is I determine my worth by my meeting mv sales quota." The lie? I determine my worth by man-made rules.

"I love the Lord and am most aware of my spiritual gifts. I work at developing and using them. But since we moved to a new city, I seem to have no real ministry. God has put me on a shelf. Considering all Jesus has done for me, I want to continue to earn His love. I feel worthless and dejected." The lie? We can earn God's love.

Do we really believe these lies? Many of us do. We need to learn to replace these lies with the truth. We need to tell ourselves the truth.

Psychologists are all excited about a so-called major discovery called "cognitive restructing": "If a person can change his thoughts, he will change his feelings and behavior." Students of the Bible have known this for some time. Our thought patterns determine our actions. Change our thinking, and our behavior will follow. Change our behavior, and our feelings will follow. This all sounds so basic, but are we living as if we believe it? Where do we go for the truth?

## GARBAGE CANS OF THE WORLD

Robert and I were staying at a small hotel in London. We checked in late so our room was not exactly in the best location. The bathroom window faced an alley. Exhausted from our overseas flight, we immediately went to bed. Around three in the morning I woke up, unable to go back to sleep. As I sat up and read in the quiet of the night, I heard a rattling noise outside the window. I held my breath. There it was again. Clink, clank, clatter! With all the bravado of a "scaredy cat," I crept in slow motion to the bathroom window. There was a man rummaging through the garbage cans. Aha, I thought. Material for a spy thriller! I was appalled at what I saw next. The man was frenziedly looking for food, and actually eating it! Had I not been reading my Bible this whole scenario might have been totally lost on me. But I thought, That's just what we do. We're digging around in the garbage cans of the world, looking for sustenance. Sometimes we even think the meal is satisfying, but inside we are starving for real food. No wonder we have a problem with our identity. Look where we find it! The garbage cans are full of the lies the world offers us. Only the "Bread of Life" will satisfy our hunger.

Here are some of the lies I dug out of the garbage:

If I could just make the pompom team, that would be "It!"

Marriage—that's "It!"

A husband would fulfill the deepest yearnings of my heart.

My husband didn't want me, and I was convinced no one else did either.

Can't you read the Bible just once?

I couldn't be a real Christian. I wore makeup, bleached my hair, and loved to laugh.

I wasn't a sinner, but a good person. I didn't murder, steal, or hijack airplanes.

God grades on a curve.

God will send me to Africa if I commit my life to Him.

You're not drunk; you've just been overserved.

I'm not selfish, just looking out for number one.

It's not really adultery, but a beautiful, meaningful relationship.

I must earn approval and acceptance from others to be of any value.

What I do is who I am.

My performance is the best measure of my self-worth.

My self-esteem depends on outward beauty.

Contentment with my body can only be found in plastic surgery.

My self-worth comes from my net worth.

I should have had perfect parents.

I'm a born loser.

Names will never hurt me.

I don't try because I know I'll fail.

I trust my emotions for my self-worth.

I'm a hopeless case.

If people serve no useful purpose, are inconvenient, are no longer attractive, and take up space, get rid of them.

There is no absolute truth.

I must drag the baggage of my past with me.

The most accurate view of myself is what others see.

My identity is one of a victim.

I choose to stay in an unhealthy and dangerous situation because I don't deserve any better.

I have no real potential.

I am inadequate. I'll never amount to anything.

I'm a negative person.

I can't change.

Have you personally confronted any of these lies with the truth of Scripture? Has your thinking changed since the first chapter? Are you beginning to see what God sees? Our worth depends on God and God alone. He says we are worth the life of His Son Jesus Christ. That's world-shaking, heart-breaking truth.

## WHAT IS TRUTH?

So what is truth? Who possesses it? When Jesus was brought to Pilate, He told him, "Everyone who is of the truth hears my voice" (John 18:37). Pilate replied, "What is truth?" It was the question of a frustrated cynic who did not stay around for the answer, but left the room. He didn't really want to know. Truth was standing right before him, but he never opened his eyes. We cannot know who we are or our intrinsic worth apart from knowing Jesus Christ. The only one who possesses absolute truth is Jesus Christ, and He said He is the Truth. The truth can set us free as Jesus promised if only we face the lies we've believed and fight them with the truth.

## THE ME GOD SEES

When I open my Bible, I find the me God sees!

I am an "Ambassador" for Christ. I am a personal messenger sent on a special mission to represent the King in this foreign land called earth.

I am the "Bride Of Christ." I have been claimed by the Bridegroom to be prepared for Him when He returns for me.

I am a "Child Of God." I have been born of God. The King is my Father. All of His resources are at my disposal. I have a great and glorious inheritance.

I am a "Citizen Of Heaven." My heavenly passport states heaven is my home and my destination. I shouldn't get too comfortable in this foreign land called earth.

I am an "Earthen Vessel." I carry the treasure of Jesus Christ in this human body of mine. God is shaping me into the character of His Son.

I am a "Faith Walking" woman. I walk by faith, not by sight, and not by fear. My faith is not in my faith, but in my God who can do all things.

I am the "Fragrance of Christ." I bear the unmistakable fragrance of having been with Jesus. Like the alabaster jar, I'm ready to be broken and spilled out for Christ.

I am "Free" in Christ. I have been forgiven of all my sins. I am free of the guilt of my past. I am not chained to the opinions of others who have kept me in bondage.

I am a "Gift" from the Father to Jesus. Jesus delights in me.

I am "God's Work of Art." God is creating value in me as a result of His love and indwelling Presence. He's making something beautiful of my life.

I am an "Heir" of God and fellow heir with Christ. What is given to Jesus will be given to me. I will suffer, but I will also share in His glory.

I am "Holy." God has set me apart for Himself, and I have consecrated myself to Him.

I am an "Image Bearer of Christ." I was created with the capacity to reflect the character of Christ. I bear the Presence of Christ within me.

I am the "Light of the World." I hold out the light of Christ to illumine, enlighten, ignite, and influence this dark and sin-sick world. I make a difference.

I am "Loved." The Father loves me just as He loves Jesus.

I am "More than a Conqueror." It is not that I will escape persecution, but because of the love of Christ, I will triumph as a "superconqueror." I can do battle with confidence because I already have victory in Jesus.

I am a "New Creation." On the cross my sinful nature was destroyed. Now that I am in Christ, I have a new nature—Christ's.

I am a "Peacemaker." As much as it depends on me, I will be at peace with and work toward peace with all people.

I am "Precious" in the sight of God. He treasures me. He honors me.

I am a "Reconciler." God has reconciled me to Himself through Jesus. I have been given the ministry of reconciliation to others.

I am of the "Royal Priesthood." I have direct access to Jesus. I intercede in prayer for others. I offer the sacrifice of praise to my God.

I am a "Runner in a Race." I lay aside sins that hinder me in the race. My eyes are fixed on Jesus. I do not choose the course I run, but Jesus has set it out before me.

I am the "Salt of the Earth." I sprinkle myself about to flavor, preserve, purify, create thirst, and melt hard hearts in society. I make a difference.

I am "Saved." I am saved from eternal separation from God by faith in Jesus. I am saved daily by the power of the Holy Spirit to overcome sin.

I am a "Servant." I am first a servant of Christ, to please Him. Next I am a servant to others, to please God.

I am a "Sheep." My Good Shepherd knows me and calls me by name. He lays down His life for me.

I am a "Soldier" in the army of the Lord. My struggle is not against flesh and blood but the schemes of the Evil One. I have access to the full armor of God in battle.

I am a "Temple of the Holy Spirit." The Spirit of God dwells in my body. I am not my own; I have been bought with a price. I will glorify God with my body.

I am a "Witness" of Jesus Christ to the world. I am to live and speak in such a manner that my life gives testimony to Christ in me.

This is who believers are and more! (See the end of the chapter for a more complete list.) We did not become these things by hard work. We did not earn these lofty titles by living a perfect life or fulfilling a list of requirements. We are who we are because God said so. We are not worthless, useless, pointless, aimless, meaningless, purposeless, or valueless. Satan has deceived us in our search for identity. The world has done a number on our self-worth. We have fallen into the traps and believed the lies. It is time to tell ourselves the truth. Only Jesus has the words of eternal life, salvation, and truth.

Dr. Chris Thurman, Ph.D. at Minirth-Meier Clinic made this important observation:

> There is a direct, inescapable connection between our self-esteem and whether or not we are dedicated to truth. If dedication to truth characterizes our way of living, we develop stable positive feelings of worth. The moment we wrap our lives around lies, genuine feelings of self-worth are virtually impossible. We've all had moments in our lives when we suddenly

saw that something we believed to be true was false. Instantly, the truth cuts like a knife. The writer of Proverbs wrote that as a man 'thinks in his heart, so is he.'[1]

## TRUTH CHARACTERIZES OUR LIVING

He was the last one to be hatched and from quite a large egg too! It was so much bigger than the ones from which other ducklings emerged. The ducks all said that it had to be a turkey egg. When he finally did peck his way out of the shell, the mother duck commented, "How big and ugly he is. Could he possibly be a turkey chick?" After she saw him swim, however, she knew he was no turkey. He had potential. He was quite a wonderful swimmer. It's just that he was so ungainly, unsightly, and unlovely. Every animal he met said he was an ugly, hideous creature. It must be so. How could he know any different? How could he know he was a cygnet?

Spring finally came, and he found himself in a large garden by the lake. He decided to approach some beautiful white swans and bowed his head before them. That's when he first saw it! The truth! The reflection? "Could it possibly be me? I'm no longer a clumsy, loathsome, ugly duckling. I'm a swan! That's who I really am. I'm different now. Maybe it's not so bad to have been born with the ducks, if you're hatched from a swan's egg."

We've all heard the Hans Christian Andersen story of the ugly duckling, but did you ever ponder over the comment about being hatched from a swan's egg? Once the cygnet saw who he really was and realized his royal heritage, it made all the difference to him. Had the cygnet's mother been there she would have told him that one day he would become a magnificent swan. She would not only have seen him just as he was, but as what he would in fact become. She knew his potential. She would have told him the truth about himself. Surely he would have believed her since mother swans know what cygnets grow up to be.

Do you know your destiny? Whom you will "grow up" to be? When people, circumstances, and events seem to call out names to us like failure, inadequate, and incompetent, why would we think any differently? Answer. Because we have a God who sees what we will become, not just what we are experiencing today. We are a creation from the Master Designer's hand. Sometimes we might think we've been born with the turkeys, but God says we are of Him. He knows our potential, our aptitude, our capacity, our weaknesses, and our strengths. He is more than adequate for whatever is facing us today. Our Lord knows the end from the beginning and everything in between.

## GOD IS IN THE NAME-CHANGING BUSINESS

God often changed the names of His people. He knew what they would one day become, as in the case of the apostle Peter. Peter's name had been Simon son of John, but Jesus said, "You will be called Peter which means, the "Rock" (Matthew 16:18).

Peter—that big, burly, Galilean fisherman—was impulsive, impetuous, immature, impudent, and most definitely imperfect. He was anything but a "Rock." His mouth was a constant source of trouble since he invariably put his tongue into gear before his brain. The only time he opened his mouth was to switch feet! I can relate.

There was the night of the Last Supper when Jesus spoke of his death and resurrection and how the "sheep shall be scattered." The "Rock" protested, "Even though all may fall away, yet I will not. Even if I have to die with You, I will not deny You!" (Mark 14:29, 31). What Jesus knew and Peter did not was that very night he would deny Jesus three times before the cock crowed twice. Peter had much to learn.

It takes a lot of work to make a rock out of quicksand. God knew what it would take. The "Rock" was indeed being formed and molded. God was about His business of transforming lives. Peter failed many times in his life. He stumbled, he faltered, he blundered, and he wept bitterly for his failings. Oh how like us he was! How like granite he became! Jesus knew what Peter would have to experience in order to become what He had planned. The Lord knew all along the kind of "Rock" Peter would become. After all Jesus named him, just as He did you.

God has been continually working on the destiny and purpose in His people's lives. Look at the year 1256 B.C. in the history of Israel. Because of their own disobedience, God's chosen people had become the victims of the oppressive Midianites. A cry of despair and helplessness went up from Israel to the Lord. God had a mighty plan to use a most unlikely individual to accomplish an enormous task. He chose to use a young man named Gideon, whom we find hiding from the enemy in the bottom of a winepress sunk deep in the earth, where he is threshing wheat. Grain was usually threshed out in the open air where the wind would blow the chaff away, but in those dangerous days it was best to stay hidden.

Gideon was afraid of being seen by some keen-eyed Midianite. He was trying to save his neck and provide for his family at the same time. No doubt about it, Gideon was scared and wanted no surprise visits. He stopped for a moment, looked up, and there sat the angel of the Lord who then said to him, "The Lord is with you, O valiant warrior." Gideon must have been thinking, "Who is he talking to? I've been threshing wheat too long. Must be the heat in here." Gideon was well aware that a valiant warrior would not be in this place.

God saw the man he would become and addressed him by his new name and identity. Was Gideon valiant? No. Was he a warrior? No. God was going to demonstrate His power at work in a weak vessel. Just as He does with you and me. Sometimes God chooses the most unlikely people to accomplish great and mighty tasks. Did you notice that God chose Gideon to be a mighty warrior, not the other way around?

## Seedlings Turn Overnight to Sunflowers

My daughter Shannon recently planted a garden at our home. I picked up the sunflower seed packet and stared at the incredible flower displayed on it. The seeds, of course, don't look at all like the plant. They're small, dry, and look quite inadequate for the grand flower pictured on the front. The packet states these will be stately sunflowers and will provide eye-catching beauty first and then later, seeds for roasting or feeding the birds. These seeds can be dried and planted and will reproduce themselves. Each plant will bear one spectacular huge bloom. I thought, Wow. This is exactly what it's going to look like.

All the potential for this enormous flower is in this very ordinary looking seed. All we need to do is plant it, water it, give it a suntan, and it will amaze us with its grandeur and benefits. Just a few sunrises and sunsets, seedlings turn overnight to sunflowers. Don't you see? We are like that sunflower seed. God breathes physical life into the seed. He continually holds the picture of our eye-catching beauty in the palm of His hand. He names us as His own. He sees clearly who we will become. All of our potential was planted in us before our birth. The Lord is well aware that sometimes there will be dry hot winds, raging spring storms, and pests trying to ravage the growing seed. He has made provision for such adverse circumstances. Sometimes great misfortunes come. Even though sunflowers have their stalks broken from time to time, they still continue to grow. God then breathes His Spirit into the growing seed as it "bends its knees" to Him. We are different now. We are not the same. He has given us a new identity, a new name, a purpose and destiny.

## SOMETIMES WE NEED A PUSH

There's a story of a dramatic rescue on an ocean cruise. When a violent storm came up without warning, a woman who was walking along the deck lost her balance and fell overboard. Many people stood around paralyzed with horror, but no one tried to help her. Suddenly a man made a nosedive into the water. He held on to her until a lifeboat came to rescue them. Everyone on board was shocked when the identity of the rescuer was made known. It was an eighty-year-old man!

A party was held in his honor to celebrate his heroism. The guests called out, "Speech, speech!" The old man was considering the rescue as he slowly stood up and said, "I just want to know one thing. Who pushed me?"

Occasionally we need someone to push us into deep waters to encourage us to swim. Are you swimming, or do you need a push? My hope and prayer is that somewhere within the pages of this book the Lord spoke to you. Perhaps it was just a word or a story but it was the push you needed to begin your journey to truly discover the person God sees!

May I encourage you to celebrate your true identity? If we listen carefully, we will hear God speaking words of affirmation and acceptance through human throats. Often they will be our own. May God give you a new "travel song" along the rough places in the road. Sing it with all your heart!

## LOVE NOTE TO GOD

Father, I have learned so much about who I am, who I thought I was, and who you see me becoming. It is overwhelming! Carve these truths on the walls of my mind. Help me never to forget them. Teach me to walk, live, and love as only You would have me do. With my whole heart I desire to become all you have meant for me to be. Comfort me with Your Spirit during the difficult lessons. Strengthen me with Your power when I am weak. I desperately need Your grace and Your love. Teach me a new "travel song."

Love,
All the me you see!

## TELLING YOURSELF THE TRUTH

1. In the list "the me God sees," what name or identity do you have the most trouble believing? Why? Have you ever been told the contrary?

2. What is the most foolish lie you have believed about your self-worth? Who told you? What identity or name in the Bible will crush that lie?

3. Do you think the truth ever hurts? Share a situation from your own life. Do we ever use lies to escape pain? Give an example.

4. How can doubting be beneficial? Do you think God may want us to doubt what we hear? Why? How can doubt help you know why you believe what you believe?

5. Were you ever told a lie you desperately wanted to believe? Why did you want to believe it?

6. Think of a situation you blew all out of proportion. What expressions or words did you use in your mind to respond to it? What could you have said to yourself? Would that have made a difference in your perception?

7. Do you believe your life is a result of the choices you make? Why? Do you believe your attitudes determine your life? Why? How do we develop right choices and right attitudes?

8. "Your attitude should be the same as that of Christ Jesus" (Philippians 2:5, NIV).

How would you describe Christ's attitude? How is it possible for us to have the same attitude?

9. How do we limit God and His truth in our lives? Is believing the truth the same as practicing it?

10. Make a list of your God-given identities that are most meaningful to you. Know it! Believe it! Live it!

## HAVE YOU MADE THE CHOICE?

Have you ever entered into a personal relationship with Jesus Christ? Perhaps you may realize you have some unfinished business to do with God. Or maybe you walked away from God years ago and you would like to recommit your life to Him. If what you've just read speaks to your heart, if you sense God irresistibly drawing you to Himself, then what would keep you from giving your life to Him? The night I gave my life to Jesus, I said the following prayer; perhaps you are now ready to do the same.

> Dear Jesus, I know I am a sinner, I have acted independently of You. I confess I have done things "My Way." I have made a decision to turn away from my sins and turn to You. Jesus, I believe You are God just as You have said. You died for my sins and rose again from the dead so that I might live eternally with You. Come into my heart. Come into my life and live in me. Make me all the person You have planned for me to become. Thank you for forgiving me my sins, and for coming into my life.

If you said this prayer with heartfelt sincerity to the God of the universe, then you are now His child. You are now a bearer of His identity. You will never be the same again. God has called you and named you!

# THE ME GOD SEES

| | |
|---|---|
| Ambassadors | 2 Corinthians 5:20 |
| Blameless | Colossians 1:22 |
| Branches | John 15:5 |
| Bride of Christ | Ephesians 5:25-27 |
| Brothers | Hebrews 2:11 |
| Called by His Name | Isaiah 43:7 |
| Children of God | 1 John 3:1, Romans 8:15b-16 |
| Chosen Ones | John 15:16 |
| Citizens of Heaven | Philippians 3:20 |
| Complete | Colossians 2:10 |
| Earthen Vessels | 2 Corinthians 4:7 |
| Elect | Mark 13:27 |
| Faith Walking People | 2 Corinthians 5:7 |
| Fellow Workers | 1 Corinthians 3:9 |
| Fragrance of Christ | 2 Corinthians 2:14-16 |
| Friends | John 15:13-15 |
| Free | Romans 6:18; 8:2; Galatians 5:1 |
| Forgiven | Colossians 3:13, 1 John 1:9, Acts 10:43 |
| Gift | John 17:6 |
| God's Workmanship | Ephesians 2:10 |
| Heirs | Romans 8:17 |
| Holy | Colossians 1:22 |
| Honored | Psalm 91:15 |
| Image Bearers | Genesis 1:26 |
| Light of the World | Matthew 5:14 |
| Living Stones | 1 Peter 2:5 |
| Loved | John 17:23 |
| More than Conquerors | Romans 8:37 |
| New Creation | 2 Corinthians 5:17 |
| Partakers, Divine Nature | 2 Peter 1:4 |
| Peacemakers | Matthew 5:9; Romans 12:18 |
| Precious | Isaiah 43:4 |
| Reconciler | 2 Corinthians 5:18 |
| Redeemed | Ephesians 1:7 |

| | |
|---|---|
| Regenerated, Renewed | Titus 3:5 |
| Royal Priesthood | 1 Peter 2:5, 9 |
| Runners in a Race | Hebrews 12:1-3 |
| Saints | Philippians 1:1; 4:21-22; Romans 1:7 |
| Salt of the Earth | Matthew 5:13 |
| Saved | Romans 10:9-10 |
| Servants | Galatians 1:10 |
| Sheep | John 10:14-15 |
| Soldiers | 2 Timothy 2:3 |
| Temples of Holy Spirit | 1 Corinthians 3:16; 6:19 |
| Witnesses | Acts 1:8 |
| Works of Art | Ephesians 2:10 |

# NOTES

Chapter 1. THE MASTER DESIGNER CAPTURES MY HEART
1. St. Augustine, *Saint Augustine Confessions* (New York: Penguin Books, 1961).

Chapter 2. WINNING THE WORLD'S APPROVAL
1. Naomi Wolf, *The Beauty Myth* (New York: Doubleday, 1991), 89.
2. Wolf, *Beauty Myth*, 119.
3. Wolf, *Beauty Myth*, 114-115.
4. *Mademoiselle* (November 1988): 254.
5. Ibid.
6. Ann Landers, "Just a Housewife," *Chicago Tribune*, 23 July 1988.

Chapter 3. BRAND NAMES
1. Leonard R. N. Ashley, *What's in a Name?* (Baltimore: Genealogical Publishing Co., Inc., 1989), 37.
2. Linda Francis, John Hartzell, and Al Palmquist, *What's in a Name?* (Minneapolis: Ark Products, 1976), introduction.
3. Norman Vincent Peale, *Power of the Plus Factor* (New York: Ballantine Books, 1987), 58.

Chapter 4. THE DESIGNER'S CREATION
1. Fay Angus, "A Designer Original," *Guideposts* (October 1992): 13.

Chapter 6. THE FEW, THE FREE, THE FORGIVEN
1. Dr. James Dobson, *Low Self-Esteem Among Adults* (Colorado Springs: Focus on the Family, 1987), 10.
2. *Big Book, Alcoholics Anonymous* (New York: Alcoholics Anonymous World Services, Inc., 1976), 335-341.

Chapter 7. FAITH WALKING PEOPLE
1. Norman Vincent Peale, *The Amazing Results of Positive Thinking* (New York: Ballantine Books, 1959), 53.

Chapter 8. THE KING IS MY FATHER

1. Brother Lawrence, *The Practice of the Presence of God* (Old Tappan, NJ: Fleming H. Revell Company, 1958), 36-37.

2. David Watson, quoted in *Fear No Evil* (Wheaton: Harold Shaw, 1985), 135-136.

3. Bruce Larson, *Luke*, vol. 3 of *The Communicator's Commentary*, (Waco: Word Books, 1983), 127.

Chapter 9. SET APART EXCLUSIVELY

1. *Zondervan Pictorial Encyclopedia of the Bible*, vol. 3 (Grand Rapids: Zondervan Publishing House, 1980), 178.

2. Max Lucado, *In the Eye of the Storm* (Dallas: Word Publishing, 1991), 232.

3. Charles Colson, *Born Again* (Old Tappan, NJ: Fleming H. Revell Company, 1972), 117.

4. Mother Teresa, *My Life for the Poor* (New York: Harper & Row Publishers, Inc., 1985), 12-13.

5. Dr. Renald Showers, *Behold the Bridegroom Comes!* (Philadelphia: Philadelphia College of Bible).

Chapter 10. DIFFERENCE MAKERS

1. Tim Hansel, *Holy Sweat* (Waco: Word Books, 1987), 119.

2. *Unger's Bible Dictionary* (Chicago: Moody Press, 1979), 956.

Chapter 11. TELLING YOURSELF THE TRUTH

1. Dr. Chris Thurman, Ph.D., *The Lies We Believe* (Nashville: Thomas Nelson Publishers, 1989), 168.